Stories from Welsh History

by

ELISABETH SHEPPARD-JONES

Illustrations by John Shackell

JOHN JONES

STORIES FROM WELSH HISTORY

© Elisabeth Sheppard-Jones 1990

First edition May 1990

Illustrations by John Shackell

ISBN 1 871083 55 9

Main distributors: Welsh Books Centre,
Llanbadarn Industrial Estate, Aberystwyth

Printed by John Penry Press, Saint Helen's Road, Swansea

Published by
JOHN JONES PUBLISHING LTD
Borthwen
Wrexham Road
Ruthin
Clwyd

Contents

Illustrations

Dedication

*This mixture of Fact, Fiction and Legend
is dedicated to my great nieces,
Helen, Elisabeth and Victoria*

The Dream of Macsen Wledig

In the days towards the end of the Roman occupation of Britain, there lived a Roman called Maximus. The Welsh called him Macsen Wledig (Wledig meaning in Welsh lord or noble), and said he was a wise and handsome man who ruled from Rome. They told a story about him that became a legend. It seemed that, when on a hunting expedition from Rome, Macsen rested in the heat of the midday sun and, under a shady tree, he fell asleep. He had a curious dream and this is what he dreamed.

He was moving slowly along a deep valley when he came to a mountain as high as heaven itself. He climbed the mountain with more ease than he had expected and, when he reached the top, there in front of him, stretching as far as the eye could see, was a land of great beauty. He climbed down the mountain and reached a wide river over which he swam and then followed its course until he came to the mouth of the river where it reached the sea. There was a great city built there and in the city Macsen could see a great castle. And also at the mouth of the river was a fleet of ships. One of these ships was bigger than the rest and had planks not of wood but of gold and silver and the bridge of the ship was of pure ivory. Macsen climbed aboard and away sailed this beautiful ship over the sea until it came to an island and here again was the mouth of another river and beyond it is a range of mountains and a stretch of woodland. Macsen disembarked from the ship and there, in front of him, he saw another castle, even more magnificent than the one he had seen before.

As the gate of the castle was open, Macsen walked through it and into the great hall where the roof was of gold and the walls encrusted with jewels. There were couches and chairs around the hall and these were of gold and, in front of them, were tables of silver. At one of these tables two red-haired young men were playing a game of gwyddbwyll which was a Welsh board game, something like chess. These lads were both dressed in black brocade and their bright hair was held in place by crowns in which sparkled diamonds, rubies and emeralds. Beyond them was seated an old man in a chair of ivory and

The Dream of Macsen Wledig

on his arms were gold bangles and on his fingers, gold rings. He was carving figures for the game of gwyddbwyll and did not look up when Macsen moved towards him. Bemused by the splendour of this place, it was a short time before Macsen's eyes settled on the far end of the hall and there, facing him, was a maiden of such beauty that she was as dazzling as the brightest sun. She was wearing a robe of pure silk and a cloak embroidered with jewels and pearls. She rose to meet Macsen, almost as if she was expecting him. He threw his arms round her and rested his cheek against hers. As he was about to kiss this lady whom he now loved with all his heart, his hunting dogs, who had been lying at his side beneath the tree under which he slept, began to bark, ready again for the chase, and their barking, together with the clang of the spears of his huntsmen, awoke Macsen from his dream.

For many days and many nights Macsen could think of nothing but the maiden of his dreams. He neglected his work and his play, his friends and his servants. One of his best friends decided he must speak to this sad ruler of Rome.

'What ails you, Macsen Wledig?' he asked.

'I am sad because of my dreams. I am happy only when I am asleep and can see my love again. Perhaps it is best that you send for the wise men of Rome for I badly need their help.'

This was done and Macsen told them of his dream and of the maiden whom he loved.

'Lord, this is what we advise,' said the leader of the wise men. 'Send out messengers to all parts of the earth until they find the land of which you dream and the castle in which lives this maiden of whom you speak.'

Macsen did as was suggested. For one year, his messengers scoured the lands far and wide. Finally, they came to the mouth of the first river about which Macsen had dreamt and to the second where was the island. Then they found the castle of Macsen's dreams and the two young men playing their game and the old man carving the figures and they saw a lovely maiden whose name they discovered was Elen. In fact, they had travelled through Italy and across France, over the island of Britain, across Britain to the west which was Wales and found the castle of Caernarfon.

9

'Behold!' cried the messengers, 'we have found that which our master saw in his dream.'

Then they explained to Elen the reason for their coming and said that Macsen's great wish was to marry her.

'If indeed he loves me,' Elen's reply, 'let him come and tell me this himself.'

By day and night the messengers travelled back to Rome where they gave their master the news of their success.

Immediately Macsen set out with them over the sea and the land. When he came to Wales he instantly recognised the fair country he had seen only in his dreams. There was the castle and the young men and the old man and, above all, looking radiant, was the lovely Elen. He threw his arms around her and, that night, they were married.

Macsen, on his journey, had conquered Britain and Elen asked as her wedding dowry that the land might be given for her father to rule over, and Macsen built two more castles for his bride, one at Caerleon and one at Carmarthen. For seven years Macsen and Elen lived in Wales but, on the eighth, they went back to Rome where a usurper had taken Macsen's place. With the help of his wife's brothers, two red-haired young men, Macsen regained Rome.

Later, when Macsen had unhappily been killed in battle for France, Elen returned to Caernarfon where she gathered around her many strong men of arms to protect Wales from attack by the Irish in the west and the Scots in the north. Elen became famous by her exploits and many a road or 'sarn' was afterwards called Sarn Elen in her memory.

Some of this story is legend; a little of it is fact. It is hard to tell which is which. It is certain the Maximus or Macsen existed as one of the last rulers of Roman Britain, and it is probable that he married Elen and that they lived together for many happy years.

The Poet

Dafydd, son of Gwilym, lay on his back on the bank of a meadow and gazed at the sky. It was spring in Cardiganshire, the county of his birth, and the date was sometime in the middle of the 14th century. Dafydd spent much of his time wandering through Wales, reciting the poems he loved to write in the great halls of high-born people. He was of noble birth himself and had little need to earn his living, which was why he could spend the whole of this lovely April day, looking and thinking and composing. A blackbird was singing in a tree nearby; 'the dark singer of the woods with a beak of coral,' Dafydd described him. Overhead a flock of geese flew past. Dafydd had once likened snow flakes to the feathers of the wild geese.

A smile crossed the poet's face as he recalled what had happened the night before. He had been at a local inn where he had met a beautiful young girl. Dafydd was the first to admit that he loved the ladies! He had introduced himself; she had been enchanted by his fine manners. He treated her to a good meal and good wine.

The meal over, 'Meet me here later,' begged Dafydd, 'when everyone has gone to bed and I will recite to you some of my poetry.'

'I don't know about that', came the reply. 'My father is staying here and would not be pleased for me to meet you late at night.'

'Please do as I ask, please,' begged the poet and so merry were his ways and so handsome his looks that the maid gave in.

'All right, I'll meet you in the room yonder in about an hour'.

The hour passed slowly; the dining room was empty and in darkness. Finally, Dafydd arose and made his way to the farther room. So eager was he to see the fair maiden that he fell in the dark; his leg struck a stool, his head hit a trestle table and a huge brass pan clattered to the floor. Unknown to Dafydd, three men – Hickin, Jenkin and Jack – were asleep in the room and hearing the terrible noise, they awoke and jumped out of bed.

'Robbers!' shrieked Hickin.

11

'Murderers!' shouted Jenkin.

'Help!' cried Jack.

Dafydd lay where he was, praying that he would not be found and, when the hue and cry was over, he slipped out of the inn. His safety was more important to him than a lover's meeting.

There, in the meadow, he smiled again at the memory of his escapade, and slowly he arose from the mossy bank. A wood nearby beckoned him as there he expected to meet another of his loves. As he was wandering among the trees, he stopped to watch a magpie building its nest.

'You should be at home by the fire,' said the magpie to Dafydd, 'not walking about in my wood.'

'Leave me alone,' snapped Dafydd. 'It is none of your business but I happen to be on my way to meet a pretty maiden whom I love.'

'You stand no chance,' replied the magpie. 'Such talk about a pretty girl! You fool yourself.'

'If you are so clever,' retorted Dafydd, 'give me some of your valuable advice.'

'I'll give you good advice,' mocked the bird. 'You don't deserve to win the love of a pretty maid. Go to a monastery, become a monk and forget about loving women. That's my advice.'

Dafydd left the scene of the argument, later to write a poem about the incident in which he said should he ever find a magpie's nest again, he would smash all the eggs.

At the far side of the wood, the lady Morfudd was waiting for Dafydd. She was one of two loves who meant more to him than any other. Morfudd was gay and enchanting and wholly unreliable. Dafydd called her 'a glowing ember'. After greeting each other, Morfudd placed a garland of beech leaves on the poet's head.

'There! I have crowned you king of the woods and king of my heart,' laughed Morfudd.

Dafydd drew her to him. 'Why then did you not marry me?' he asked.

'Because I married someone who could give me more security than you could,' came the answer.

'But to marry the Little Hunchback – Y Bwa Bach – it was

ridiculous of you. I don't know that I ever want to see you again.'

Dafydd had often said this before to Morfudd but he always changed his mind. Morfudd's moods, too, often changed. She did not always welcome Dafydd and once she left him standing in the cold and sleet, refusing to open the door for him. She took the jewels he gave her and was delighted by the thirty poems he had written to her but she flitted from one lover to another which made Dafydd's friends tease him for his foolishness in loving her.

Now, in the wood together, they talked and laughed and kissed, and reminded each other of the lack of fidelity. Indeed, Dafydd was no more faithful than Morfudd.

The other great love of his life was called Dyddgu. She was a lady of as noble birth as Dafydd himself. She was virtuous and clever and highly regarded by all who met her. Dafydd courted her to no avail. She never professed love for him; she remained polite, cold and distant. Like the twelfth century troubadours before him, Dafydd wrote her flattering and highly romantic verses – eight poems in all. He did not consider himself good enough for her but he dared to hope that, when she tired of her other suitors, she might accept him as her husband. She never did and, no doubt, in time, he forgot her. But his poems to his two loves, Morfudd and Dyddgu, ensured that Wales never forgot them. Dafydd ap Gwilym is to the Welsh what Shakespeare is to the English – a great national poet.

The Feud

Fulke Fitzwarren was only seven years old when his father decided to send him to one Joce de Dinan of Ludlow Castle. The young boy cried, sulked and begged to be allowed to stay at home but it was the custom of the day to send boys to a household where they might learn to be knights and trained to be good soldiers. In the days of the Middle Ages there was much fighting and quarrelling among the many noble families who lived on the border of Wales, and Fulke's instructor Joce de Dinan had had a long feud with a family called de Lacy.

For many a long year, Fulke stayed at Ludlow, returning to his family for short periods every now and again. There had been for some years an uneasy peace between Joce and the de Lacys but matters changed abruptly when Fulke had just celebrated his seventeenth birthday. Early one summer morning Joce and Fulke had climbed to a high tower in the castle, as they did daily, to look out for any trouble there might be in the lands around.

'Quiet as usual, Fulke,' said Joce, as they mounted the stairs together.

'Indeed I hope so, my lord,' replied Fulke as they reached the battlements.

The lord and the boy looked towards the south where stretched peaceful green fields in which grazed cattle and sheep. But then they heard a great noise in the distance. Quickly the couple looked towards the north where it was far from peaceful. Approaching the castle was a large army, banners flying and armour glinting in the sun.

The alarm was quickly sounded and the castle instantly became a hive of activity.

'Go below and stay with the ladies,' Joce ordered Fulke.

The boy began to argue but Joce insisted that he was too young to join in the fighting.

At the head of 500 knights, men at arms and local townsfolk (or town burghers as they were called) Joce marched out to meet the de Lacys, for it was his old enemy who now attacked him.

The battle went well for Joce and many prisoners were taken.

The Feud

It was Walter de Lacy who had led the enemy forces and it was he Joce most wanted to capture. In the confusion this de Lacy had been cut off from his men and Joce saw him turn round and ride off on his horse. Joce mounted his own horse, and alone, began to chase after de Lacy. He caught him while still in sight of the castle and dragged him to the ground. De Lacy was about to submit when three of his knights appeared suddenly and, in defence of their lord, set upon the unfortunate Joce de Dinan.

Now Joce had two lovely daughters, Sybil who was dark as a raven and Hawyse who was as fair as a swan. Leaving Fulke in their quarters, the girls had gone to the castle battlements to watch the battle raging below. They saw to their horror what was happening to their father and their shrieks of alarm brought Fulke hurrying to the scene.

'What is the matter, Sybil? What ails you, Hawyse? I understand the battle is going well for us.'

'Alas, alas!' cried Sybil, 'our father is at this very moment being attacked by three of de Lacy's knights and there is no-one near to help him.'

'And where were you, brave Fulke, when you were needed,' asked Hawyse in an accusing voice.

'In your quarters where your father ordered me to be,' said Fulke.

'You are nothing but a wretched coward,' said Sybil, 'hiding like a baby in the ladies' quarters.'

'It was not my fault; I did as I was told,' Fulke defended himself.

'A man with more courage in his heart would have disobeyed such an order,' said the fair Hawyse.

'I'll show you that I am a brave and noble knight,' shouted Fulke, unable any longer to bear the reproaches of the two maidens. And he rushed down the stairs into the great hall, clapped on his head a rusty helmet that was lying there and seized an axe which was the only weapon to hand. He then rushed to the stables and mounted an old worn-out nag, and arrived just in time as Joce was being overwhelmed by Walter dy Lacy's men. Fulke smote the first knight, felling him to the ground; then the second knight he cut in two with his axe. The third knight he hit on his helmet of white steel until it split in half. This last man was a near relation of Walter de Lacy, by the name of Arnold and, although Fulke had wounded him, he was not killed. He and Walter de Lacy were taken to the castle by some of Joce's men who had now arrived on the scene.

Sir Joce turned to Fulke who, with the visor of his helmet down, was not recognisable.

'Friend burgher,' said Joce, 'you are strong and brave and, without your help, I should now be a dead man. I am grateful to you and from this day on you may live with me and I shall be your protector.'

'Sire, do you not recognise me?' asked Fulke and removed the rusty helmet. 'I am Fulke Fitzwarren for whom you have cared during many a year.'

Joce was astonished. 'My son, it was a good move I made when I consented to take you as a pupil. You have amply rewarded me.'

The two important prisoners, Walter de Lacy and his kinsman Arnold, were treated with courtesy and kindness. Arnold was a particularly handsome man and it was not long before Sybil was charmed by his attentions to her. Indeed, she agreed to marry him.

'But I can only do so when you are a free man and welcomed as such by my father,' she told him.

'Help me and my cousin Walter to escape then,' implored Arnold.

After some persuasion, Sybil agreed to help him. She used the familiar method of knotting sheets together and the two nobles climbed out of her bedroom window and departed from the castle.

The next morning Joce arose early and, seeing that all was well as he surveyed the countryside, he descended into his apartments to wash himself and to eat his breakfast. He called for his prisoner, Sir Walter, to join him for so high did Sir Joce regard Sir Walter, he would never wash nor eat without him. His knights and servants searched the castle and the vast grounds but nowhere could the prisoner be found. Unexpectedly, Sir Joce did not worry much about this but his generosity was not returned and there continued to be skirmishes between Sir Joce and Sir Walter.

17

There was peace for a while and this was when Fulke married Joce's daughter Hawyse. He had always been fond of both daughters but it was Hawyse whom he loved. She had apologised to him for her accusation about his cowardice and he had kissed her pale cheek and professed his love.

'We shall be married here at Ludlow which is more home to me than anywhere else in the world,' he promised her, 'and the Bishop of Hereford shall perform the ceremony.'

There followed many days and nights of merrymaking and celebration, after which the whole family party left for a visit elsewhere. Thirty knights and seventy soldiers only were left to guard the castle against possible attack by the de Lacys. Sybil, too, had decided to remain in Ludlow, in spite of the entreaties from her sister and brother-in-law that she should go with them on their prolonged honeymoon. Sybil stayed behind for a good reason. She wanted to see the man she loved, Sir Arnold Lacy and, when the others had departed, she sent word to him, telling him that the window through which he and Sir Walter had escaped would be open and that he might visit her at any time.

Arnold apparently did not love Sybil as much as she loved him. He realised that a visit to her might offer an opportunity for him to conquer the castle while Joce de Dinan was absent. Sybil had sent her lover a silk cord that she usually fastened round the waist of her gown. It was the exact measurement from her window to the ground. Arnold chose a cloudy, moonless night to keep his assignation. He brought with him a light leather ladder but, more important, he also brought with him a thousand armed men whom he bade to remain hidden until he told them otherwise.

'Sybil,' he called softly, 'Sybil my beloved, I have come to you. My ladder is the exact length of the silk cord you sent me.'

Sybil appeared at the window, her heart beating at the sight of the man she loved. At his bidding, she fixed the top of the ladder firmly against the sill of the window and Arnold climbed up it and into her arms.

While Sybil and Arnold talked of love, the ladder remained where it was against the wall. As daybreak approached, a hundred of de Lacy's men stealthily climbed the ladder. A sentinel was hurled from the watch tower and those knights and soldiers who had been left behind were slaughtered in their beds. Then the gates of the castle were opened and the rest of the de Lacy men poured in – and the castle was theirs.

Meanwhile, poor Sybil, aghast at what had happened and stricken by Arnold's treachery, seized his sword and plunged it into Arnold's heart. He died at once and Sybil clung to his dead body, rocking herself to and fro in her sorrow.

'Oh, Arnold, how I loved you,' she sighed, 'how could you have behaved so badly to me? Through my foolish love for you, my family has been betrayed and I wish to live no longer.'

With these words, she arose and moved to the window. The courtyard below was full of jostling soldiers. Sybil gave one last sigh, took a last look at the man she had loved so much, and threw herself out of the window.

Of course, later Fulke Fitzwarren and Joce de Dinan had their revenge on the de Lacys for the death of Sybil and the men who died in the castle but nothing was ever solved and the terrible feud between them continued to cause further deaths and unhappiness.

The Fairy Wife

Here is another story from the borders of Wales and it concerns a Saxon rather than a Welshman. His name was Edric and his is a strange, legendary tale.

Edric was the Earl of Shropshire, having gained this honour through his service to William the Conqueror. He changed his allegiance to the border Welsh and began to harry the Conqueror's men who lived in the Border country. Not having much success with them, he went back to William and fought with him against the Scots. He was obviously not a man to be trusted; he led a stormy life, fighting first with one group of men and then with another. But his greatest adventure occurred on the afternoon of one winter's day.

Edric was hunting alone in the forest when he saw ahead of him a large, brightly lit-up house.

'Ah,' he said to himself, 'I am tired after hunting all day and maybe here I can get some food and drink.'

He dismounted and tied his horse to a tree. He walked up to the front door of the house and knocked twice. No-one came but he could hear the sound of laughter and music so obviously there were people in the house. He rapped on the door again, louder this time, but still no-one answered. He turned the handle of the door and, finding it unlocked, he opened it and walked quietly into the house. He stood back in the shadows of a large hall and gazed, entranced, at the sight that met his eyes.

A number of beautiful ladies, clad in white dresses of the finest silk, were dancing and singing to the music of a harp played by one of their company. Each lady had glorious golden hair that reached her waist and swung to and fro as she danced. The dance was wilder and more intricate than anything Edric had seen before. The rhythm was intoxicating and the singing, which was in a language foreign to his ears, was sweet and haunting. These fairies – for Edric was sure he was seeing magic folk – did not look like fairies who are usually said to be tiny. These were tall, bigger than human maidens. Edric knew he was seeing something strange and uncanny. At first, enchanted by the scene in front of him, Edric had not noticed that, among the fair ladies was one fairer than the rest. But now his eyes suddenly alighted on her. She was in the middle of the dancers and Edric thought he had never seen any woman so beautiful. It was love at first sight and he determined, there and then, to have her for his wife. He rushed boldly into the whirling dancers and seized by the waist the fairy he wanted. Her lovely companions stopped dancing, the harpist stopped playing. He was faced with a hostile crowd. They shouted and screamed at Edric and tore at him with their teeth and nails. But Edric was an experienced fighter and a strong man. Hitting out left and right, he dragged away his prize. Through the front door he ran and after him streamed the fairy maidens. Edric pulled and pushed his captive on to the horse, mounted it himself and rode off into the dusk. The cries of the fairy sisters finally faded away into the distance.

Back in his castle, Edric spoke kind and loving words to his fairy.

'You are beautiful beyond dreams,' he told her, 'and I loved you the moment I saw you. Can you not love me, too, and agree to marry me?'

The maiden sat still with her hands in her lap, her eyes downcast and tears like pearls trickling down her pale cheeks. She said not a word and, for three days, she continued to sulk. On the third day, Edric again addressed her.

'You are beautiful beyond dreams and I loved you the moment I saw you. Can you not love me, too, and agree to marry me?'

She lifted her eyes and looked at Edric. Her eyes were of so bright a blue, he was briefly quite dazzled by them.

'I'll marry you,' she said softly 'if that is what you want. And I will be a good wife but I must warn you about one thing.'

'What is that, my beloved?' asked Edric, hardly able to contain his excitement now that the fairy had consented to be his wife.

'Never, never refer to the place where first you saw me, nor to the scene nor to my companions for, if you do, you will lose me.'

'It shall be as if they never existed,' promised Edric.

The beauty of his bride soon became known far and wide until King William himself heard about it. He commanded Edric to bring her to court where her loveliness astounded everyone. Edric refused to answer any questions about who she was and where she came from.

'It is a secret, a secret between the two of us,' he would say and his wife would smile sweetly at him and nod her golden head.

For some years it was a happy marriage. The fairy was a good wife and loved her husband. However, she did pay occasional visits to her fairy relations and, after a time, Edric began to resent the days she was away from him. The day came when he had particularly missed her; he felt lonely; he wanted to hear her sing and to see her dance. She was longer away than she had said she would be. He felt hurt and angry and, when she finally appeared, he made a fatal mistake.

'You have been away too long,' he shouted at her. 'I do not like you going to that house where your fairy sisters live. I do not like them and I am sure they are a bad influence on you.'

As soon as the words were out of his mouth, Edric regretted them. He had done what he had promised he would not do – referred to her fairy past. Before his eyes, the form of his fairy bride began to fade away until she completely disappeared from his sight. Edric never saw her again and, a few months later, he died of a broken heart.

This isn't the end of the story, for it was often told that Edric and his fairy bride could be seen riding together through the forest, and that they appeared only on the eve of a great war and always approaching in the direction from which the war was threatened. For, example, there was an unusual sighting of them on the eve of the Crimean War, hundreds of years after the days of William the Conqueror.

A young woman of the neighbourhood was walking with her father along a country road that led through the self same forest where Edric had first met his bride. Suddenly was heard the loud blaze of a hunting horn.

'Cover your head immediately with your shawl,' said the father. 'It is not right that you should witness what is about to appear. I shall myself wrap my scarf about my eyes.'

The girl pretended to obey her father's instructions but could not resist peeping out of the shawl. She was rewarded by the sight of a strange troop moving past her and her father. In a few minutes they had gone.

'There was nothing to worry about, father,' said the girl.

'Did you look? Did you look?' asked the father in some agitation.

'What did you see?'

'A great crowd of people, ghostly grey in appearance,' replied the daughter. 'At their head were two leaders, a man and a woman. He had short dark curly hair and bright black eyes, and wore a green cap with a white feather in it, and a short green coat and cloak. A horn and a short sword hung from his belt. The lady had wonderful fair hair falling to her waist and on her head was a band of gold. She, too, was dressed in green with a short dagger at her waist.'

The girl had seen a vision of Edric and the fairy. Incidentally, these ghosts and their company have not been seen for a very long time now as they never appear in times of peace. Let us hope they will never be seen again.

The Mother of Wales

Catherine de Beraine was descended from Henry VII, her grandfather being the king's illegitimate son. Henry had made him Constable of Beaumaris and given him large sums of money. When he married the heiress of a family called Penrhin, he became very wealthy as his bride brought him a good dowry. He had only one child, a daughter who, as a wealthy kinswoman and later an orphan, was made a ward by Queen Elizabeth I. Elizabeth was young at the time and her ward, being very pretty and popular, proved too much competition to the vain queen, so she was not kept long at court. Instead, she was offered as a bride to the nobility of Wales. Maurice of Beraine won the prize and from this marriage, too, there was one child, another girl. Her name was Catherine and she was even richer than her ancestors and clever, lively and good-looking into the bargain. She married a Salusbury of Llewenny, another wealthy man, but he died young and his youthful wife went sorrowfully (or so it seemed) to his funeral.

Salusbury had had two close friends, Sir Richard Clough and Maurice Wynne of Gwydir, and both of these men were in love with Catherine. On the way to the church for the funeral services, Richard comforted the sorrowing widow.

'You will always have me to lean upon, my dear lady,' he told her.

'You are kind, Sir Richard,' replied the lady. 'I am but a frail woman and do not know how I shall manage now my husband has gone. Life is very hard.'

She wiped away her tears and put a fine linen handkerchief to her eyes. Sir Richard patted her on the shoulder.

'I have long loved you, Catherine,' he said, 'and now that you are alone, I should be glad if you will do me the honour of becoming my wife.'

This was not perhaps a very tactful moment for a proposal and one would have expected Catherine to reject his advances but Sir Richard was also a wealthy man and, rich though Catherine was herself, she was not averse to a further fortune.

'Maybe it is not right to accept such an offer when we are

24

on the way to my husband's funeral but, nevertheless, though you take me by surprise, I do accept you.'

She had accepted Sir Richard before they had even reached the church. The service over, Maurice Wynne approached the widow to offer his condolences. Taking her hand, he said to her quietly, 'This may not be the right moment but I have to declare my love for you, Catherine. Could you ever find it in your heart to become my wife?'

Catherine managed to hide a smile and dabbed once again at her eyes.

'You do me honour, Maurice Wynne,' she said, 'but I regret to say you are a little late. I have already agreed to marry Sir Richard Clough.'

Poor Maurice was amazed and shocked. He thought he had been a little premature with his offer but it had never occurred to him that he might have been forestalled. He managed to pull himself together and, taking both her hands in his, he said, 'I cannot pretend that your news has not come as a surprise and I am saddened to hear you are to marry someone else. Nevertheless, may I ask one favour of you?'

'Certainly,' replied Catherine, 'although I cannot promise, of course, to grant you what you wish.'

'Heaven knows I do not want any harm to come to Sir Richard, my rival though he is, but if by some misfortune you are widowed again, will you reconsider my offer of marriage?'

Here was yet another rich man; Catherine felt herself to be doubly blessed. She was too overcome to speak but she nodded her head and squeezed Maurice Wynne's hands.

When he was only forty years old, Sir Richard died and Maurice Wynne could scarcely believe his luck. He and Catherine were married a month or so after the funeral of her second husband. However, Maurice did not live long to enjoy his newly wedded bliss and died a few years later. Had Catherine not been highly regarded in the Vale of Clwyd where she lived, it might have seemed that she was disposing of husbands rather too quickly. No sooner was Maurice cold in his grave when she had another proposal from yet another rich man, Edward Thelwell of Plas-y-Ward. Thus Catherine had married into four of the most powerful families in North Wales·

Salusbury, Clough, Wynne and Thelwell. Her descendents from these four husbands were as the sands of the sea and thus it was that she was given the name of Mam Cymru or the Mother of Wales.

Catherine Clough's husband, the most famous of the four, did give her a little trouble. He had built for them a house near Denbigh called Bachygraig. At the top of this house was a windowless room and, in this, Richard would shut himself at night, forbidding anyone to enter while he was there. The country people believed he had conversations with the Devil. Catherine apparently had similar suspicions. The legend grew up that, on one occasion, she crept quietly up the stairs and looked through the keyhole. To her amazement, she saw her husband and the Devil chatting together. In horror, she opened the door and confronted them.

'My dear husband,' she cried, 'what are you doing in such evil company?'

'My dear wife, please do not interfere. This gentleman and I are having a serious philosophical discussion. It is of no interest to you.'

Catherine moved towards him as if to protect him from the dark stranger. The Devil glowered at her, his eyes flashing fire, and she was rooted to the spot. Then the Devil seized hold of Sir Richard and dashed right through the wall with him. Sir Richard was found, shivering in the garden, and refused to discuss the matter with his wife. After this, Catherine's life with her other husbands, Wynne of Gwydir and Edward Thelwell of Plas-y-Ward must have been comparatively peaceful!

Ellen Gethin

There lived once, in a valley in Radnorshire, a well-known family called Vaughan. One of the tales told about these Vaughan concerned one who lived just before the Wars of the Roses. Her name was Ellen Gethin or Ellen the Terrible. This makes her sound an unattractive character but she was called Terrible only because of one single act and not because her behaviour was always savage.

The home of Ellen Vaughan and her brother David was called Hergest Court and their cousins Vaughan lived at Tretower in Breconshire. As so often in Welsh history, the Vaughans had family quarrels as to which branch should be head of the clan. Now Ellen was particularly devoted to her brother and was alarmed when one day he told he was to have a meeting with Tir Sion (or Long John), a Vaughan from Tretower.

'I beg you not to go, David,' said his sister. 'Tir Sion is a dangerous man and you know how bitterly he feels towards us. Stay at home and forget about him.'

'My honour is at stake,' replied David, 'Tir Sion has asked to meet me and it would be cowardly to refuse.'

'Well then, go in peace; do not provoke our cousin but discuss family matters calmly and with dignity.'

This David promised to do and would have kept his promise had Tir Sion not been in an angry, fighting mood.

Ellen awaited her brother's return with some anxiety. He had departed early in the morning for a meeting place on the borders of Radnorshire and Breconshire. The morning passed and so did the afternoon. Ellen paced up and down the terrace of Hergest Court. The sun set, throwing long shadows across the garden, and still David had not returned. As Ellen was about to leave the terrace and go into the house, she saw two of the Vaughan servants approaching the house from the garden. They were carrying the body of a young man. Ellen put her hand to her mouth to stifle a scream and ran swiftly to the spot where her dead brother had now been laid.

'What happened, what happened?' cried Ellen, getting down

on her knees and hugging to her breast her beloved brother's curly head.

'Tir Sion Vaughan, my lady,' said one of the servants, 'lost his temper when the master suggested Vaughans of Hergest should be the head of the family. He drew his sword and pierced the heart of your brother. He did not have a chance but died instantly with no time to defend himself.'

Ellen was too grief-stricken to cry or to speak but, there and then, she vowed to have vengeance on her cousin. She did so in a dramatic fashion.

The following week there was to be a great archery competition held in the neighbourhood of the Tretower Vaughans. Ellen spent her time practising at the archery butts. She had always been a proficient archer but she needed to be perfect. Tir Sion was known to be a particularly skilful archer.

When the day of the competition arrived, Ellen dressed herself in some of her brother's clothes and tucked her hair into one of his caps. With her slim figure and thus disguised, she looked like a very handsome youth. She needed this disguise because only males could enter the competition. It was not thought right that women should be archers. Ellen slipped off across country to the gathering and arrived just in time to see her cousin fire his last and, as it proved, victorious shot.

'Well done,' she called, striding forward from the admiring crowd. 'You shoot very well, my lord.'

'Better than any other in Wales,' boasted Tir Sion.

'I doubt that,' said Ellen.

Tir Sion frowned. 'You are an insolent boy,' he said.

'Not insolent but honest, sire. I know of one who shoots better than you.'

'Why did he not appear for the competition then?' growled Tir Sion.

'Because he was too late but he is here now.' Ellen smiled at her cousin, hiding her true feelings.

Tir Sion looked about him. The crowd began to murmur.

'Bring him forth,' bellowed Tir Sion, 'and we shall see who is the better man.'

'He is here,' said Ellen quietly, 'at your side. I am he.'

28

Ellen Gethin

Tir Sion looked astonished, 'You a mere lad and think you can beat me? All right, let us see you in action then.'

'As you will, my lord,' said Ellen, fixing an arrow to her bow. Carefully she drew back the bow, released the bowstring and let the arrow fly to the target. It hit near the gold, the centre of the target.

'A good shot', admittted Tir Sion, 'but possible to beat.'

His arrow flew through the air and landed very near Ellen's arrow.

Tir Sion ran across the grass and up to the target that he might judge whose arrow was nearer to the gold.

'Nothing much in it,' he called, 'but it would seem that I am a little nearer the gold than you.'

Ellen fixed another arrow to her bow and called back, 'Maybe that is true but this arrow will not miss its target; it is for you and not for the gold.'

Tir Sion was hit in the chest and collapsed to the ground. He was dead.

'So, I have my revenge,' murmured Ellen to herself, and she ran into the astonished crowd and was lost to view. Changing into her woman's clothes and releasing her long hair from the cap, she easily escaped from the scene of her crime. No-one ever discovered who was the stranger who shot Tir Sion.

This story has a happier end. Some years passed before Ellen met Tir Sion's brother and fell in love with him. The quarrel between the Vaughans of Hergest and the Vaughans of Tretower was satisfactorily resolved. Ellen married Lord Tretower and, later the bards sang her praises in stirring verse which may be read today. We are not told if Ellen ever revealed to her husband the truth about his brother's death.

The Powells

It was not only among the Vaughans that there were family feuds. The Powells of Monmouth had their troubles some three centuries after the shooting of Tir Sion by Ellen Gethin. The Powells were actually neighbours of some of the Vaughans and, for the sake of clarity we will call them Powells of Plas A and Powells of Plas B. And they were sworn enemies.

It was about the end of the 18th century when Thomas Powell of Plas A invited an English guest, names Charles, to spend some time with him in Wales. They had been spending a merry day in the town of Monmouth, eating and drinking well at a local inn, so it was rather later than intended that they called for their horses to take them back to Plas A.

'Not a good night, Charles,' said Thomas Powell, 'perhaps we should have started out earlier.'

'Perhaps,' agreed Charles who seldom spoke as much as his voluble friend.

It was raining hard as they left Monmouth and they had not ridden many miles before there was a shaft of lightning, followed by a clap of thunder and the rain increased in force. Drenched and miserable, the couple rode on.

'A thousand apologies, friend, for bringing you out in such rough weather,' said Thomas.

'Not your fault,' grunted Charles.

They rode on in the darkness, the storm increased and Thomas Powell began to feel sorry for his friend and not a little for himself.

'I am looking forward to hot food and a warm hearth,' he said, trying to be cheerful. 'It's foul weather we are having to be sure.'

'Not unusual for Wales,' came the cold reply.

'Plas B is not far from here,' said Thomas, 'and we could seek comfort there. It is a misfortune that the Powells of Plas B are not on good terms with the Powells of Plas A, but we could at least give it a try.'

'Really, what an extraordinary situation!' exclaimed Charles. 'You Welsh are always fighting with your relations.'

'Well, it stops life being too dull,' said Thomas. 'Actually, I think, on this occasion, we might reasonably seek shelter with my cousin. He could not refuse us hospitality on such a night as this.'

Soon they arrived at Plas B. The house was in darkness. Thomas Powell knocked hard on the door. There was no reply. He and Charles began to shout. Cousin Powell was awakened from his sleep by all the tumult. He threw open his bedroom window and called down, 'Who is it? What do you want so late at night?'

'It is I, your Cousin Thomas. We have been caught in this dreadful storm. Surely you will not refuse shelter to me and the English friend who is with me?'

Cousin Powell of Plas B reacted well to these words. Charles was somewhat surprised at the warmth of his welcome.

'Certainly, Cousin, certainly. I'll be down in a minute to let you in.'

Suddenly the window was re-opened. 'Just a minute, Cousin Thomas,' said Cousin Powell. It has just occurred to me that, now I have offered you hospitality, you can no longer refuse to recognise that we Powells of Plas B are the head branch of the Powell family.'

There was silence from Thomas. Charles nudged him. 'For heavens' sake, man, agree to his terms.'

Thomas shook his head. 'No, no, I cannot do that,' he called up out of the darkness and pelting rain. 'I will do anything else to oblige you, Cousin, but not that, not that. The Powells of Plas A have always been head of the family.'

There followed a tremendous argument between the two Powells that went on for an hour or so. Charles could not believe what he was hearing. He tried to quieten them.

'Enough, enough,' he said, 'this is neither the place nor the time for such a silly discussion.'

But neither Powell took any notice of him and both went on with their tirade. Finally, Cousin Powell shouted, 'Well, well, I'm sorry, Cousin Thomas, but if you will not acknowledge my claims, I cannot offer you hospitality.' And he slammed down his bedroom window.

There was nothing Thomas and Charles could do. They

re-mounted their horses and wearily made the long journey back to Plas A. Charles had been horrified by the whole incident.

'This is the last time I stay with any Powells who live in Wales,' he told his host. He started to cough and splutter. 'What's more, I think I've caught pneumonia.' However, it turned out to be only a bad cold and he soon recovered. He returned, as soon as possible, to England where his own relations all lived in peace with each other.

Mary Jones and the Bible

It was the end of the 18th century; Mary Jones was eleven years old and was paying a visit to her friend Bethan Evans who lived in a cottage next door. The two girls had been playing on the floor of the kitchen-living room when Mary suddenly looked very serious.

'Bethan, your mother and father are not as poor as my parents, are they?' she asked.

'I don't know,' replied her friend, 'they are quite poor, I think or we should not be living in this wretched hovel. Dada is only a farm labourer like your father.'

'But you have something we do not have and which I should dearly like.'

'And what can that be?'

'Go on, have a guess; it's something in this room,' teased Mary.

'A rug on the floor? A special tea set for Sundays? A patchwork quilt that Mam made?'

To all these suggestions Mary shook her head. 'Come on, Bethan, I'll give you a clue. It's on a shelf and it's something very precious.'

Bethan's eyes rested on a shelf above the fireplace. 'I can only see a china dog and an old clock – and I know you have both of those in your house. Oh yes, and there's a book there, too.'

'Right, and that book is a new Welsh Bible if I'm not mistaken. We can none of us read English but I can read Welsh.'

'I'd forgotten, of course you can read,' said Bethan. 'I don't know how you learnt as neither of us has ever been to school.'

'I have an uncle who can read and write,' said Mary proudly, 'and he taught me. Bethan, do you think I might just look at your Bible?'

Bethan was uncertain. 'Oh, I don't know, Mary. It has never been taken down from that shelf as none of us can read. Father bought it last year and, like you, Mam thinks it a precious book.'

'Please, please,' implored Mary. 'I won't damage it. I'll handle it very carefully.'

'Oh, all right then. I suppose Mam won't mind.'

Bethan reached for the book and handed it to Mary. Mary was about to open it when Bethan's mother came into the room.

'Mary Jones, what are you doing with that holy book,' she demanded to know.

'She's only looking at it, Mam – and she can read, you know.'

'I'm sorry,' said Mary, 'but I've never seen a Welsh Bible before, although I do know many biblical stories. I persuaded Bethan to let me see it, so please don't be cross with her.'

Mrs. Evans patted Mary's head. 'Go ahead, my child and, if you will read some of the book to me from time to time, I should indeed be grateful.'

Mary smiled happily and began to read from Genesis while Bethan and her mother listened quietly and marvelled that one so young and uneducated could reveal such wonders to them.

When it was time for Mary to return to her own home, she asked one, important question.

'Can you tell me, Mrs Evans, how much the Bible costs?'

'About five shillings, my dear – a whole week's wages. I was angry at first that Mr. Evans should spend so much money on a book but, if you will read to us from time to time, I shall think it was money well spent.'

Bethan went to the door with her young friend. Mary looked thoughtful.

'One day, Bethan,' she said, 'I am going to buy my very own Welsh Bible.'

'How will you ever have five shillings, Mary. It is a fortune for the likes of us.'

'I'll get it. I'll save the money however long it takes me,' said Mary. 'You wait and see.'

That night when Mary was tucked up in her trestle bed, her mother came to her.

'You look as if that head of yours was in the clouds, my girl,' said Mrs. Jones, 'and not at all as if ready for sleep.'

'I'm thinking, Mam, how long it will take me to save five shillings.'

'Five shillings!' exclaimed her mother, 'What do you want with so much money?'

'One day I'm going to buy a Welsh Bible.'

Her mother laughed. 'Go to sleep, Mary, and put such foolish thoughts out of your head.' She kissed her daughter and told her to have a good night. But Mary did not have a good night. She made plans. The next day she earned her first half penny.

It took all of Mary's courage to face the Lady of the local Manor the next day. Fortunately she could be seen through the large iron wrought gates leading into part of the vast garden and Mary was thankful that she did not need to go up to the front door and risk a rebuff from one of the haughty servants. She pushed open the gate and timidly approached the Lady, who looked up from her weeding of a crescent-shaped flower bed.

'What do you want, child? Who are you?' she asked quite kindly.

'I'm Mary Jones and I should like to earn a penny. I'm quite useful. I'll do anything you want – wash dishes, scrub floors; I can even bake bread like my Mam taught me.'

The Lady smiled and got up off her knees. 'Well, you must understand, Mary, that I have a staff of servants to do all those things. And I do not think they would like it if I employed you, too. Tell me why you want a penny.'

'To buy a Welsh Bible, my lady,' came the swift reply.

'Surely you cannot buy a Bible with one penny.'

'No, it costs five shillings but I don't mind how long it takes me to earn it. One penny would be a beginning.'

The Lady was impressed but could think of no way Mary could earn her first penny at the Manor.

'I'm sorry, child, but really there is nothing for you here.' She put her hand to her back and groaned a little. Mary seized an opportunity.

'You are stiff, my lady, from the weeding. I could weed this bed for you – for a penny. I do know weeds from flowers, honestly I do.'

Rich though she was, the Lady of the Manor liked to make a bargain. 'You are right, I am stiff but the weeding is worth only half a penny.'

'I'll do it,' said Mary, adding quickly, 'I could weed other flower beds too.'

The Lady shook her head. 'The gardeners look after everything else. I tend only the rose bed as it is my particular favourite. Well, don't let's stand here talking. Get on with the work and earn your money.'

That first half penny was as valuable to Mary as anything she had ever had and, when she reached home she found a small box into which she carefully placed the coin. It was the first step.

It was to take Mary five more years before that box was to contain the five shillings she needed. She took any small job she could find but there wasn't always anything available as the village of Llanfihangel y Pennant where she lived was both small and poor. She ran messages; she looked after children; she washed steps and, that first summer, she had high hopes of earning something at hay-making time. Unhappily, her father worked for a farmer who was notoriously mean and, although Mary toiled in his fields day after long day, the farmer grudgingly gave her only one penny at the end of the season, saying he did not expect to pay anything at all when families of his labourers helped out. 'Food and drink is provided and that is all,' he said, 'so consider yourself lucky, Mary Jones.' And he would not, he said, nor did not give her a penny in succeeding years.

During the five years that went by Mary occasionally borrowed the Bible from next door and, every now and again, she would read parts of it to Bethan and her mother. Mary's own mother was of the opinion that Mary would never get a Bible of her own and sadly watched her daughter getting thinner and paler with the work she did, when and where she could get it.

On her sixteenth birthday Mary's father gave her the final penny. Mary could scarcely believe her luck. She counted the coins in the little box three times before she was sure she actually had the five shillings.

Bethan was working as a scullery maid at the Manor, a job Mary herself would have liked but did not hear about until it was too late. Mary now ran to the Manor and around to the back door which led into the huge kitchen where Bethan was scouring out some pots.

'Bethan, Bethan!' cried Mary, throwing her arms round her friend and causing her to drop a pan with a clatter on the floor.

Mary Jones and the Bible

'I've done it! At last I've done it! I have the money for the Welsh Bible.'

'Did you come all this way, interrupting my work, just to tell me that,' said Bethan crossly.

'No, not exactly. I want you to tell me where your father bought the Bible.'

'In Bala, I think – no, I'm sure,' replied Bethan.

'Bala!' The smile left Mary's face. 'But that's twenty five miles away.'

'It's the nearest place where they sell books, I know that,' said Bethan. 'I know that, and I know you can buy a Bible from Mr. Thomas Charles who holds a Sunday school in Bala. You could get a lift from the carter when he goes to market, couldn't you?'

'Yes, of course, I could but he charges two pence for the journey.'

'Well, wait then until you've earned the extra money.'

'Oh, Bethan, you don't understand. I've waited all these years and now I have the necessary five shillings, I can wait no longer.'

'What will you do then?' Bethan could not understand Mary's eagerness to buy a book full of words she herself could not even understand.

'I'll walk,' said Mary, 'that's what I'll do. I'll walk.'

'Walk, twenty five miles! And you so small and thin. And, oh! Mary, you don't even have shoes on your feet.'

But Mary was adamant and told her parents what she had already told Bethan and both her mother and father remonstrated with her as Bethan had done. The next morning, Mary set out in the dawn of what promised to be a fine day, on the long journey to Bala. At first, she skipped along the country road, her spirits high and her steps light. She began to feel hungry and thought she would stop and rest a while to eat the bread and cheese which her mother had supplied. Then she changed her mind; she would eat as she walked and thus save time. By mid-day her pace had slowed; the sun was so hot she felt her cotton dress sticking against her shoulders and her bare feet, although accustomed to being shoe-less, had begun to ache. She had seen only a few farm labourers working in the fields and one shepherd herding his sheep from one hillside to another. In mid-afternoon she met a milkmaid who gave her a welcome mug of fresh, frothy milk and, in the late afternoon, a cottager offered her a cup of water and a piece of currant cake.

Dusk approached and Mary just managed to see, through the gloom, a signpost at a crossroads which told her it was still twelve miles to Bala. She had walked thirteen miles that day; she was exhausted and her feet burned as if on fire. She knew she could go only a little further. Ahead of her, she saw a barn and towards this Mary made her weary way. It contained only hay and, with relief, she sank down into it and fell asleep. She was awakened early next morning by the sound of rain on the barn roof. It was welcome after the heat of the preceding day and, after eating the last of her bread and cheese, Mary set out again on her long walk. It was her wet clothes which now clung to her small body and, as the weather got worse, Mary could see only a few yards ahead of her. On she struggled, up hills and down dales, the thought of the Welsh Bible soon to be hers, urging her on.

It was seven o'clock at night by the time Mary reached the outskirts of Bala. She was cold, hungry and exhausted, her bare feet bloodstained and blistered and she was at the point of collapse when she managed to say a few words to a man who was pulling a cart of vegetables.

'Can you tell me, please, sir, where I might find a Mr. Thomas Charles?' By a lucky chance, the man was both kind and helpful.

'Yes, miss, I know where Mr. Charles lives and I'll be passing the very place. You look fair worn out so up you get on top of the cabbages, and I'll take you up there.'

And so Mary, at last, reached her goal. Needless to say, Thomas Charles was amazed at Mary's story. He sold her the Bible and arranged for her to stay the night with some of his friends. She actually stayed a couple of days until her feet were sufficiently recovered to make the journey back to Llanfihangel. She returned as she had come but taking longer this time, resting her body now and again by the roadside and, refreshing her spirit by reading her new copy of the Welsh Bible.

So impressed were the people of Llanfihangel by the determination and courage of this young girl that, many years later, they put up a monument to her memory which can be seen to this very day.

Owain of Powys

Cadwgan, Prince of Powys, who lived in the 12th century, had a son Owain of whom he was proud until the boy grew into manhood. The man proved to be reckless, wild and argumentative. Poor Cadwgan's troubles started at a festival in Cardigan where the lord of Powys also ruled. As was usual on such occasions, a bard sang to the harp for the entertainment of the company. It was then that Owain first heard of the lovely Nesta. The bard sang of her beauty, her sweetness, her kindness and intelligence; in short, she sounded a perfect woman.

'I would have such a lady for my wife,' said Owain to his father.

'Put thoughts of Nesta out of your mind, my son. She is married to Gerald de Windsor of Pembrokeshire and has two children, and she is a model wife.'

'I could steal her away,' laughed Owain. 'That would be something of a joke, would it not?'

Cadwgan frowned. 'Such a subject is not to be joked about and such action might cause endless strife.'

'I was not being serious,' said Owain but nevertheless he had been fired with the idea of abducting the fair lady and, later that evening, he discussed the idea with a group of his closest friends. Only one of these tried to dissuade him.

'Sire, do you know who is the father of this lady?'

'No, but why should that bother me?' asked Owain.

'Because he is none other than Rhys ap Tudor, Prince of South Wales. Added to which Nesta is King Henry's ward. There might be no end to the fighting were you to displease either of these mighty men, not to mention Gerald himself who loves his wife beyond all else.'

'A good fight is what we need to liven up our dull lives,' smiled Owain. 'Life has been too quiet for too long. Who comes with me to Pembrokeshire will be well rewarded.'

All, except the friend who had warned Owain, agreed to go with him. So it was that at dead of night, this band of ruffians approached the castle where Gerald and Nesta lived. They dug under the huge gates at the entrance of the castle and crept one by one through the tunnel they had made. Safely inside the courtyard, Owain brandished a torch with which he set alight the gates. There was instant confusion in the castle at the sight of the fire. Taking advantage of this, Owain left his men to cope with Gerald's soldiers and found his way into Nesta's bedroom. There, proudly facing him and clutching her two children by each hand, stood the most exquisite woman Owain had ever seen. She was frightened by both the noise and this daring intruder but she moved not a muscle.

'What are you doing here and where is my husband?' she asked coldly.

'I have come for you,' replied Owain, 'and I do not care a damn where your husband is.'

In fact, Gerald was not showing much bravery; he had climbed down a drainpipe and escaped as soon as he realised his men were outnumbered by those of Owain.

Owain now seized Nesta by the wrist and pushed aside her weeping children. Nesta tried to fight him off but he was strong and she was no match for him. She did manage to scratch his face with her nails at which he cried out, 'Ah, I see we have a tigress here and I well like a woman who shows some spirit.' And he pulled back her head by her long black hair and kissed her on the lips. She shuddered and hoped that Gerald or one of his men would soon come to rescue her. She hoped in vain for the men who now entered her room were Owain's men and all nearly as wild as Owain himself. There was nothing Nesta could do and, to protect her children, she quietly submitted and she and they were carried off to Powys, where they were kept prisoners in a hunting lodge called Plas Cadwgan in the Vale of Llangollen.

If Owain had wanted some fighting, he now had more than enough. His escapade brought down on his head the combined wrath of Nesta's Kinsmen and of the King himself. His abduction of Nesta, the 'Helen of Wales' as she was later to be called, caused as much turmoil as did the abduction of Helen of Troy by Paris.

It was Owain's father Cadwgan who suffered most. When the fighting became general, he was forced from his lands and even lost the lordship of Powys, while his son fled to Ireland, leaving behind Nesta and her children. Cadwgan was finally restored to his possessions but soon his impossible son started a fight again and, again, Cadwgan paid for the sins of his son. He was killed in battle while Owain lived to reign over Powys and to serve the King with distinction in Normandy.

How long Nesta was kept in custody we do not know but we know she finally managed to find her way back to Pembrokeshire. Many years had passed but Gerald of Windsor did not forget the wrong that had been done to him. He awaited an opportunity to get his revenge. The time came when he and Owain were serving the King against a rising in South Wales. They were comrades in arms and it never occurred to Owain that Gerald would wish him harm for Owain had a short memory and had forgotten how enchanted he had once been by Nesta's beauty. One day, when out riding on his own, he saw Gerald approaching, accompanied by some of his men.

'I see you are alone, Sire,' said Gerald. 'It is not usual to see you without your retainers.'

'It is good sometimes to be alone; it gives one time for thought,' replied Owain cheerfully.

'And do you think about your past misdeeds?' asked Gerald.

'Sometimes, but I don't regret the life I've led and would apologise to no man for my sins.'

'You would not apologise to me then for the wrong you once did me and for abducting my wife and children?'

'Oh, that is old history. Let us not quarrel about that. Indeed it was a fine adventure at the time but I had almost forgotten it.'

'Well, I have not,' retorted Gerald, signalling to his men who instantly released a shower of arrows into Owain's body. He fell from his horse and lay dead on the ground. Gerald had had his revenge.

The Wreck of the Spanish Galleon

Many ships have been wrecked off the coast of Wales and one particular hazard is a place, on the Gower Coast, called Worm's Head, a promontory which stretches out to sea. This rocky, dangerous spot has always struck terror into the hearts of seamen and is in strong contrast to the peaceful sandy bay of Rhosilli which lies off it.

In 1625 a Spanish galleon, loaded with gold, struck the rocks and drifted on to the deep sands of Rhosilli. It was a wild night, the waves crashing on the shore and the wind howling like a banshee but, remarkably, the crew all managed to get off the ship without harm or loss of life. The captain suggested to his men that they take as much gold as they could carry and leave the scene quietly without rousing suspicion. The dark stormy night made it difficult for the men to load themselves with many sovereigns but they stuffed what they could into their pockets. Then they slipped away into the night.

The next day, the captain was drinking at an inn when he met a man called Thomas.

'Judging from your accent,' said Thomas, 'I would guess you are a stranger in this country.'

The Spaniard nodded and, without more ado, boldly asked, 'Are you interested in buying a wreck?'

Thomas was very interested. 'Where is it?' he asked.

'Rhosilli Bay and safely beached on the sand.'

'And how much are you asking?'

'Not much to a gentleman like yourself,' replied the Spaniard. 'Name a figure.'

For an hour or so they argued over the price but finally Thomas handed over a bag of sovereigns and the wreck was his. The captain forgot to tell Thomas what the ship had been carrying and Thomas, having had a few drinks, forgot to ask. Indeed, for a time, he forgot he owned a wreck and, by the time he remembered, the ship had sunk too deep into the sand for him to be able to break it up.

Every now and again, as the years went by, someone on the beach would come across a gold piece and thus word got around

44

The Wreck of the Spanish Galleon

that the wreck was a treasure ship and Talbot, Lord of the Manor, put in a claim for it. Nothing further happened until fifty years later when Mansell, another Lord of a Manor who had no actual rights to it, came to Rhosilli one night and got away with a hoard of gold. Fearing the Talbot's wrath, he went abroad where he died, apparently, a rich but unhappy man, made guilty by his crime. It was said his ghost returned to the scene where it drove up and down the shore in a black coach with four grey horses. A descendent of the ghostly Mansell had better fortune as the result of a wreck. Mansell of Margam was the local Lord of the Manor and, in 1787, a vessel carrying orange trees was wrecked on the nearby coast. The trees were apparently a gift for the King of England from the King of Portugal and this cargo was claimed by Mansell as his manorial right. The orangery, which can be seen to this day at Margam Abbey, is said to be the largest in the world.

Early in the nineteenth century, the Rhosilli wreck, which had been invisible under the sand for a long time, suddenly re-appeared on the occasion of a particularly low tide. This time the crew of a smuggling boat landed on the beach and took a fortune from the wrecked galleon. They were seen doing this by a couple of local people and soon the news spread around and hoards of people descended on the Bay. Not only the locals appeared but strangers, too, from some distance away. Eager and greedy for gold, the two factions started fighting on the beach. Talbot, as true Lord of the Manor, soon put a stop to the rioting and decided that he himself would examine the wreck, and a proper search was made. Still more dowlone were discovered before the wreck again disappeared, only to re-appear the following year to reveal more gold than ever. It was then that a descendent of the original Thomas arrived on the scene and faced Mr. Talbot.

'I have more right to this wreck than you,' this Thomas said, 'and the gold should be mine.'

'How is your claim better than mine?' asked the Lord of the Manor.

'In that my ancestor bought the wreck off a Spanish captain two hundred years ago .'

'A long time ago and much has happened since then, and

I would remind you that I am Lord of the Manor and therefore have rights to any ship wrecked on my coast.'

A bitter argument followed until, finally, an angry Mr. Talbot said, 'Enough of this; the wreck has caused me nothing but trouble. You shall not have it and I will not have it. Here and now, I give all rights to the people of Rhosilli. And that shall be the end of the matter.'

So it was that after that time, the local people continued to take little hauls of coins until the treasure finally came to an end.

The Wreckers

Through marriage, the Vaughans of Carmarthenshire inherited Dunraven Castle of Southerndown, on the coast of Glamorgan, and there they lived quiet and worthy lives until the early part of the 17th century when a certain Walter Vaughan inherited the property. He was a profligate and a spendthrift and there came a time when he did not know how to pay his debts. So he took to ship-wrecking as a means of improving the family fortunes. He was introduced to this horrible form of crime when, as a magistrate, he ordered a man called Matt to have his hand cut off as a punishment for piracy. Later this villainous character was known as Matt of the Iron Hand as he wore an iron hook fastened on the stump of his wrist.

Having heard in court of Matt's evil deeds, Walter Vaughan decided that here he had found a possible partner in crime. He sent for Matt to come to the castle and there he questioned him. The squire sat at a table and Matt stood, glowering, on the other side of it.

'Now, what I have to say to you, Matt, is in the strictest confidence. I need money and I think I need you. You were condemned for piracy; do you know anything about wrecking?'

Matt gave him a suspicious look and growled. 'Don't know what you're talking about to be sure; I pleaded innocent to the piracy charge and I'm certainly innocent of ship-wrecking.'

The squire smiled sardonically. 'Come on, Matt, I know better than that. You don't fool me with talk of innocence. You were guilty as hell of piracy and I suspect you are equally guilty of wrecking. But I also suspect, from the look of you and the hovel in which you live, that you have not been too successful.'

Matt shuffled his feet and said nothing as he tried to decide if he could trust the squire or not.

'Now I have a good scheme which put into action could be of great benefit to both of us,' went on Vaughan. 'But first I must have your answer. Are you an experienced wrecker and will you join me?'

Matt shook his large, shaggy head and muttered something under his breath.

'Speak up, man,' said the squire. 'If you don't agree to my plan, well, that's an end of it.'

Matt again shuffled his feet. There seemed no harm perhaps in trusting Walter Vaughan who was already known in the area to be something of a devil.

'I dunno sire, we'd need more men than you and me. And, anyway, wrecks round here aren't that many. Too much is known of the dangers.'

Vaughan now knew that Matt was going to trust him. 'There could be more wrecks, a good many more, the way I've worked it out. And, surely you know a few men as villainous as yourself, who would come in with us.'

'Well, to be honest with you, sir,' said Matt who was seldom honest about anything, 'I have had a hand in wrecks down the coast and I do know a couple of men – Dic Thomas for one – who have worked with me in the past.'

'Right, that settles it; I can see you're willing and I know you're experienced. My idea is this. In the past, there have been occasional wrecks in the bay of Southerndown, usually on the notorious rocks of Trwyn-y-Witch.' Trwyn-y-Witch – Nose of the Witch – was a rocky promontory to the east of the bay and, like Worm's Head, a dangerous spot for seamen.

'There is a way to lure sailors on to these rocks,' went on the squire.

'Praying for storms is the only way I know,' grunted Matt.

'My way is better than prayer,' smiled Vaughan. 'We tie lights on to the heads of my cattle who graze on top of the cliffs. Sailors will mistake these lights for those of a safe harbour, Cardiff perhaps. Of course, it will have to be a stormy night and preferably one without a moon. The captain will steer the ship inland and on to the rocks where you and a handful of men can grab any cargo you can lay your hands on.'

'And kill the crew or those who are not already drowned. Dead men tell no lies.' Matt grinned to show blackened teeth, recognising in the squire the evil he had in his own heart.

After some further discussion, in which the Squire said he would not always be present at the wrecking but could see to

49

the distribution of any valuable cargo, the two villains parted, and Matt set off to find a few friends who had themselves as little conscience as the two chief plotters.

In the winter months that followed, ship-wrecks increased in the bay, mostly on rough nights, as the wretched sailors mistook the lights on the cattle for the lights of a harbour and were thus lured onto the cruel rocks. There, awaiting them, was the wicked gang headed when possible by the Squire and by Matt when his master was engaged on more lawful business. No sailor ever left the scene alive, and the cargo that was saved made Vaughan a rich man, able at last to pay his debts.

Walter Vaughan had long forgotten the time he had ordered Matt to have his hand amputated but Matt was constantly reminded of it by the iron hook and, as his bitterness increased, so did his determination to get his revenge whenever the opportunity arose. One night, when the wind howled, the rain lashed down and the sea was like a boiling cauldron, the Squire saw to it that, as usual, lights were fixed to the heads of his animals and they were let loose to roam the heights above the bay. Matt and his men but not, on this occasion, the Squire, hurried to the beach. Coming up the Channel was a large ship, carrying rich cargo from France. As it was battered to and fro in the wild sea and misled by the lights, the captain guided the ship towards the Trwyn-y-Witch and it crashed, with a tremendous roar on to the rocks. The shouts and cries of Matt and his companions mixed with the shouts and screams of the sailors as they disappeared into the sea. The few who had managed to scramble on to the land were pushed back to drown with their mates. Matt's men began to pull out of the water the floating barrels of wine and the protected bales of silks and satins. Matt himself was peering at the face of one of the drowned men whose body had been washed up on to the shore. By his dress, it was obviously the captain of the ship, and on a closer inspection, Matt let out a shout of triumph. He was looking at the dead body of Squire Vaughan's favourite son who had been away at sea for two or three years.

'At last I'll make that Squire sorry he ever met me,' grunted Matt to himself and, taking out a knife from under his sodden jacket, he cut off the hand of his victim and put it into his pocket.

A couple of hours later Matt presented himself at Dunraven Castle and was shown into the study where the Squire was looking at his accounts book and congratulating himself on how much the wreckers had made of late. He scarcely looked up as Matt approached him.

'We've done well,' he said, 'and how did it go tonight? I heard the noise. Did you retrieve any cargo? And was it worth anything? Last time you didn't manage to produce anything but a few barrels of rancid butter.'

'Ah, 'twas a good haul tonight, sire,' leered Matt, 'that I can tell you. We'll all have money in our pockets when you've handled this little lot.'

'And no-one left to tell the tale, I hope,' said Vaughan, pushing aside his accounts book.

'On my soul, not a one, Squire. I myself saw the captain dead. And I've proof of that right here.'

With these words, he produced the hand of Vaughan's son, on the index finger of which was a signet ring with the Vaughan crest on it.

The Squire took one look at it and let out a wild cry of despair. 'My son, that's my son you murdered, you brute. What use of riches when my son is dead? Leave me alone, Matt of the Iron Hand, that I may mourn in private. Our wrecking days are over.'

Matt silently withdrew, a small smile of triumph on his lips. As he left the castle, he could still hear the Squire's cries of sorrow and regret. Maybe the organised wrecking would now cease without the Squire at its head but Matt had had his revenge and was satisfied.

The terrible shock of realising he had indirectly killed his own son unhinged the already unbalanced mind of Walter Vaughan. He sold his property, left Southerndown and was never seen again.

51

Saint Melangell

Brochwel, Prince of Powys during the 8th century, was fond of hunting, especially in the lovely country around Llangynog in North Wales. On one occasion, he and his men were enjoying a day's sport when they saw a particularly fine hare racing across a field in front of them.

'Follow the hare!' cried Brochwel as one of his huntsmen blew the hunting horn. The great array of men, horses and dogs immediately began to move in the direction of the animal. The hare's speed increased and so did the speed of the huntsmen. Temporarily the quarry was lost as the hare darted into a copse but it was not long before the dogs picked up its scent but, once among the trees, the dogs suddenly came to an adrupt halt. They began to whine and howl but refused to move.

'Urge on those dogs,' ordered Brochwel but, although the huntsmen cracked their whips and called to them, the dogs still refused to move.

'Well, we'll go on without them,' shouted Brochwel, angry with the obstinate dogs but puzzled also at their strange behaviour. He and his men and horses pushed on until they came to a clearing in the wood where, kneeling at prayer, was a beautiful maiden and, peeping out from under the hem of her dress, was the hare they had been hunting.

'There it is, sire,' cried one of the huntsmen. 'There's the hare!'

'Go and get it then,' said Brochwel. 'It will make a very fine supper dish, to be sure.'

The dogs had moved even further away and now the horses were neighing and shivering with fright. The young girl finished her prayer and rose to her feet, still guarding the hare.

'Do not touch this hare; he is under my protection,' she said coldly, looking Brochwel straight in the eye and showing no fear.

At a nod from Brochwel, one of the huntsmen lifted his horn and was about to blow it, when he found the instrument had stuck to his lips. Some of the other huntsmen began to laugh but Brochwel gazed at the maiden in astonishment.

'Have you put a spell on us, my lady, just to save the life of one small hare?' he asked.

Saint Melangell

She said nothing but only inclined her head.

'It is a miracle,' announced Brochwel. 'And what, fair lady, do they call you?'

'My name is Melangell and I am an Irish princess,' came the reply.

Brochwel addressed his huntsmen. 'The hunt is off,' he said, 'no-one shall hunt the hare.' Then he asked Melangell what she was doing in Wales to which she replied, 'A marriage was arranged for me to a man of ill-repute and bad honour. I came here to escape from him and have lived here in the copse for fifteen years; you are the first human I have seen in all that time.'

'And have you not been lonely and unhappy?' Brochwel spoke gently to her.

'No, I have had the animals and I have communed with God. It is a peaceful life. I have no regrets – well, perhaps just one . . .'

'And, pray, what is that?' asked Brochwel.

'I should dearly have loved to build a church to the glory of God but, alas, I have no lands nor wealth with which to do this.'

Brochwel was deeply moved by this devout lady and, after a few minutes' thought, he said, 'I own all the land hereabouts and it is in my power to give to you the land at Pennant and the money for both a church and a convent.'

And so it was that Pennant Melangell had its church and the maiden became Saint Melangell, the patron saint of hares. The hunt seldom chased hares in that part of the land, and the local people, if they saw one being hunted, would shout out, 'Saint Melangell protect you,' and, sure enough, the hare would always escape.

Owain Glyndwr and Lord Grey

Ruthin Castle had been built by Edward I and was later, in 1399, occupied by an Englishmen, Lord Grey, who ruled somewhat brutally over the surrounding land. He was a typical medieval baron, exacting dues and taxing traders and markets and generally making himself very unpopular with his Welsh subjects. He must also have been something of a fool and was probably the cause of the last uprising of the Welsh against the English which was led by Owain Glyndwr.

It so happened that Owain's property, which was a large one, bordered that of Lord Grey. Now Owain was a man of some importance and was the social equal of his neighbour; the Welsh possibly thought him superior as he was descended from the Prince of Powys. It is doubtful that, at this time, Owain was restless or looking for trouble but, as so often happened, he and Grey had a dispute about a boundary. During this argument, Grey seized part of Glyndwr's land and Owain decided to go to London to seek justice at the High Court.

'I wish redress from Lord Grey who has illegally seized some of my land,' Owain told the officials.

'And who, may I ask are you?' said one of the officials, 'and why should we listen to your complaint?'

'I am Owain Glyndwr,' came the answer, 'and of some importance in my own country.'

'And what country is that?' sneered the official.

'A country of great pride, a country of poets, of musicians and brave fighters. The country of Wales.'

'Oh that country!' The official sniggered. 'I am sorry but, in the circumstances, there is nothing we can do for you. We are not able to give you any sort of hearing. You yourself will have to settle your quarrel with Lord Grey.'

Owain, feeling himself snubbed by the English officials, decided to do exactly as they had suggested – settle his quarrel with Lord Grey in his own way.

On his return to Wales, he gathered his men about him and attacked the Castle of Ruthin, looting the town and burning much of it to the ground. Lord Grey was absent at the time but soon gathered his men about him and his army and that of Owain met at Bryn Saith Marchog. The Lord of Ruthin was defeated and captured. Captured with him was another English lord, Edmund Mortimer.

Lord Grey was one of King Henry IV's men and the King was angry at what had happened and sent an envoy to Owain, demanding news of the prisoner.

Owain greeted the envoy and treated him with the hospitality due to his rank.

'May I ask what brings you here,' said Owain. 'It surely is not to give me greetings from the King.' Owain remembered well the poor way he had been treated when in London.

'He does, in fact, send greetings,' replied the envoy diplomatically, 'but he would also like to know what has happened to Lord Grey.'

'He is imprisoned but well cared for, which is more than he deserves after his treachery to me.'

'To come to the point, my lord, King Henry wants him released as he is a loyal servant of the crown.'

Owain smiled and fingered his beard. 'Surely he does not expect me to release Lord Grey just because it suits him for me to do so.'

'He is prepared to pay a ransom,' said the envoy.

'Oh a ransom is it? And what, pray, does he think Lord Grey is worth?'

'A few thousand marks,' suggested the King's man.

'Let us be exact; let us say ten thousand marks,' snapped Owain.

'Ten thousand'. That's a fortune; I do not know that the King will agree to that amount.'

'Return to him then and say I will take no less.' Thus Owain ended the conversation.

So the envoy returned to London where the King, although appalled at the size of the ransom, finally agreed. Back the envoy travelled to Wales.

'I have brought the ten thousand marks you demanded,' he said.

'I have a further demand now,' said Owain.

The envoy turned pale. 'I do not think the King will grant anything else.'

'Then Lord Grey stays where he is and dies a prisoner.'

'I – I cannot make any promises,' stammered the envoy, 'but, perhaps if it is not too much . . .'

'I want the ownership of Lord Grey's manor in Kent,' demanded Owain.

Back to London went the weary messenger and once again received the King's consent to the demand. In Wales Owain received the news with delight. It had taken a year for the ransom to be settled and Lord Ruthin was set free. But, before the royal messenger had departed, Owain had something further to say to him.

'There has been no mention of any ransom to be paid for Lord Edmund Mortimer who is also my prisoner.'

The messenger smiled this time. 'King Henry will pay no ransom for that particular lord; you can keep him as long as you like.'

The truth was that, whereas Grey was a loyal subject of the King, Mortimer was not to be trusted for he himself had a claim to the throne. The King was quite happy to have such a dangerous rival permanently in Owain's clutches. As a result of this, Glyndwr made a faithful ally of his prisoner who was freed and married Catherine, one of Glyndwr's daughters and therefter fought by Owain's side.

The affair of Lord Grey and the King's contemptuous attitude to Glyndwr embittered the Welshman and it was then that although he was already middle-aged, he began to rouse his fellow Welshmen into rebellion against England. The Glyndwr rising was one of destructive ferocity and united many of those in both north and south Wales who had previously been at each others' throats. Now it was the whole of Wales against England. Owain's supporters called him the Prince of Wales, and for many years the fight continued unabated.

Owain was a great fighter. In his early days he had fought in both Ireland and France and also in a battle at Berwick on Tweed. His bard Iolo Goch, said that there he drove men before him with a broken spear and that the grass withered at his fiery attack. He was favoured at the beginning of his rebellion with such good luck that his followers regarded him as a magician who could even change the very weather when needed. Owain was himself a superstitious man who believed in his fortune as he read it in the stars. Owain had the support of France and of a few English nobles who were out of favour with King Henry but, by 1410, his luck deserted him and the Welsh were defeated. By now, Henry V was on the throne and twice offered Glyndwr a pardon but the old man, as he now was, refused to accept, preferring to remain a hunted outlaw.

No-one knew where or how Owain Glyndwr died. No bard sang of his death because no Welshman believed he had died. He became a national hero: one day he would again lead his people to victory. He then became a legend and, like the immortal King Arthur, it is said he lies somewhere in the Welsh mountains waiting the call to return whenever Wales should need him.

Pwyll, Prince of Dyfed

Pwyll, Prince of Dyfed, was lord over a large domain and, one day, he decided to go hunting at a place called Glyn Cuch. Early in the morning, he set off with his companions. He sounded his horn and began to muster the hunt but somehow he and the other huntsmen were separated and Pwyll found himself alone with only the pack of hounds for company. As he listened to the cry of the dogs, he heard in the distance the cry of another pack of hounds.

Now Pwyll saw a clearing in the wood and, as he reached the edge of it, he could see a stag in front of the other pack which had overtaken it and brought it to the ground. Then he looked at the dogs and, of all the hounds he had seen, these were the strangest. They were brilliantly white with red ears and as the shining white glistened in the morning sun so did the redness of their ears. Pwyll drove off the pack that had killed the stag and set his own dogs on it and, while he was encouraging them, he saw a horseman on a big, light grey horse, a hunting horn round his neck and wearing a brown garment by way of hunting dress. The horseman drew near.

'Prince,' he said, 'I know who you are but yet I will not greet you.'

'And, indeed, why not?' asked Pwyll. 'Can it be that you have too much dignity to address me?'

'It is not that,' replied the stranger.

'What then is it?'

'By God, it is your discourtesy and ignorance. You drove away my hounds which had killed the stag and put your own dogs on to it.'

'Chieftain,' said Pwyll, 'if I have done wrong, I apologise and would extend my hand of friendship in any way you desire.'

'And how would you do this?' asked the stranger.

'According to your dignity – but I do not know who you are,' replied Pwyll.

'I am a crowned king in my own land.'

'Well, greetings, then, my lord, and tell me what land you come from?'

'I am from Annwn and I am Arawn, King of that country.'

'And how may I win your friendship?' asked Pwyll courteously.

'I will tell you,' said Arawn. 'There is a man whose land borders mine who is forever warring against me. His name is Hafgan and, by ridding me of this man, you would most certainly win my undying friendship.'

'I will gladly do as you ask but only show me how I may do it,' said Pwyll.

'I will set you up in Annwn instead of me. I will change you into my likeness and I myself will look like you. You will then rule in my stead until the end of a year and a day, when we shall meet again in this very place.'

'Yes, I understand,' said Pwyll, 'but though I be in your land for a year, how shall I find the enemy of whom you speak?'

'A year from tonight,' replied Arawn, 'there is to be a meeting between me and Hafgan at the Ford. But you, in my likeness, shall go there, and you must give him just one blow and this he will not survive and, although he may ask you to deliver another blow, this you must not do.'

'I have one more question,' said Pwyll. 'What is to happen to my own kingdom while I am away?'

'I shall look after your kingdom for no – one will know I am not Pwyll, Prince of Dyfed, because my looks will be as yours.'

'Well, I shall be on my way,' said Pwyll, 'and nothing shall prevent me getting to your kingdom with you to guide me.'

All day, the two princes travelled until they reached the land of Annwn where Arawn left Pwyll. The disguised prince entered the castle which was the palace of Annwn and he saw it was handsome and magnificently built. He went into the great hall and everyone there greeted him as if he were Arawn. Squires and servants helped him off with his hunting boots and two knights removed his hunting clothes and dressed him in a robe of gold brocaded silk. Then the Queen entered the hall and she was beautiful and wearing a yellow robe of shining satin.

Pwyll was afraid that she might realise he was not her husband but, at dinner that night, she sat at his side and conversed with him in a natural and lively fashion. They passed the evening with meat and drink and song, and Pwyll thought he had never seen a court with better food and such gold and jewels. He went to his bedroom to sleep but he did not kiss the Queen goodnight, knowing he was not her real husband.

The next year was spent in hunting, feasting and singing and, at last came the day when Pwyll must see Hafgan, the enemy of Arawn, King of Annwyn. They met at the middle of the Ford and Pwyll struck Hafgan on the centre of his shield which broke into two and Hafgan was thrown to the ground for he had received a deadly blow.

'My lord,' cried Hafgan, 'strike me again and complete your work.'

But Pwyll remembered Arawn's words and refused to strike another blow.

'Tell me,' he said, 'now that you are dying, who shall be my subjects?'

'Lord,' replied the dying man, 'my lands and those of Annwyn should be ruled by no-one else but you,' and with these words Hafgan died.

Pwyll now ruled over all the land and, the next day, as he had promised, he met Arawn at Glyn Cuch, and they were pleased to see each other after an absence of a year and a day.

'May Heaven reward you,' said Arawn when he had heard Pwyll's story.

'And what then of my own country?' asked Pwyll anxiously.

'I have done what I could for you,' came the reply, 'and now I shall be myself and you shall be yourself.'

Arawn was happy to return to his own people but they, not knowing that he had ever been away, were surprised at his high spirits. He kissed his beautiful wife Rhiannon whom he had not seen for such a long time.

'Why, my lord,' she said, 'you have not touched my lips for the length of one whole year.'

And Arawn realised what a good friend Pwyll had proved to be in that he had not touched Arawn's lovely wife. Then he told her the whole of his story, and she was much amazed.

Pwyll, Prince of Dyfed, was also pleased to be home again and he began to ask his nobles how he had ruled over them for the past year.

'Lord,' they said, 'never were you so wise nor so loving, never did you rule better.'

'It's only proper,' confessed Pwyll, 'that you should know that it was not I but King Arawn, in my likeness, to whom you should be grateful for he had ruled here in my absence.'

'Thank God,' said the nobles, 'that you and he had such friendship and we hope you will continue to rule as he did.'

From that time forth, Pwyll and Arawn were good friends and they would send presents to each other – horses, greyhounds and hawks and, sometimes, gifts of jewels and treasure. By reason of Pwyll having spent a year in Annwyn and having ruled as well there, and having united the two kingdoms of Arawn and Hafgan by his courage, he was later to be known, not as Pwyll, Prince of Dafydd but Pwyll, chief too of Annwn.

Pwyll and Rhiannon

Once upon another time, Pwyll was at his place at Narberth where he was feasting with his men. After the meal, he arose from the table and went for a walk with his companions to the top of a small hill called Gorsedd Arberth.

'Did you know, my lord,' said one of the courtiers, 'that it is said that whoever sits here cannot leave without receiving wounds or blows or else seeing something wonderful.'

'I should not like the wounds or blows,' replied Pwyll, 'but I should much like to see something wonderful, so I shall sit here for a while.'

And something wonderful did happen. He saw a lady, riding a pure white horse and wearing a garment of shining gold, coming along a road nearby. The horse seemed to be moving slowly in the direction of the hill.

'My men, do any of you know that lady?' asked Pwyll.

The shook their heads, so Pwyll asked if someone would go and find out who she was.

One of the men went to the road to meet her but she passed by without looking at him and he ran after her as fast as he could and, although he was a swift runner, he could not catch up with her. The faster he ran, the further away went the lady on the white horse.

The man returned to the hill top. 'Lord,' he said, 'no-one could follow her on foot.'

'All right,' said Pwyll, 'return to the palace, take a fast horse and go after her.'

The courtier did as he was told. He came to a level plain and, ahead of him he saw the lady. He urged on his horse yet still he could not catch up with her although she appeared to be riding at a slow, steady pace. His horse began to tire so he returned to the hill where Pwyll was waiting for news.

'Lord,' he said, 'I could not catch up with the lady. I rode a fast horse but it is impossible to get near the white steed.'

'There is something strange here,' said Pwyll, and he returned to the palace until the next day when he and his men went back to the hill. Pwyll had ordered another of his men, a youth, to bring with him the fastest horse in the stable that he might be prepared to follow the lady immediately she appeared. They did not wait long before the lady on her white horse came riding by.

'There is the lady of yesterday,' said Pwyll to the youth. 'Mount your horse quickly and go after her and inquire who she is.'

The youth did as he was told but, before he had settled himself in the saddle, the lady passed by. Her speed was no greater than before. The youth trotted his horse, thinking that he could soon overtake her. But this didn't happen so he urged on his horse, but still came no nearer. Finally he gave up the chase and returned to Pwyll.

The next day Pwyll ordered his page to saddle his own horse. 'Bring it to the road and bring also my spurs.'

Again, the prince and his men assembled on the hill and they had not been there long before the lady appeared on the same road, in the same manner and at the same slow pace.

'I see the lady coming,' cried Pwyll and no sooner had he leapt on to his horse than she had passed him by. He let his horse bound forward, thinking he would soon reach her but he came no nearer to her. He urged on his horse still faster but to no avail.

'Oh maiden,' called out Pwyll, 'for the sake of him you love best, stay a while.'

The maiden stopped abruptly. 'Certainly I will stay,' she said, 'and it had been easier on your horse had you asked this before.' She threw back that part of her headdress which covered her face and fixed her lovely blue eyes upon Pwyll.

'Lady, where do you come from,' asked Pwyll, 'and where are you going?'

'I go on my own errand,' she replied mysteriously, 'but I am glad indeed to see you, sire.'

'My greetings to you lady,' said Pwyll, who thought he had never seen so beautiful a woman. 'Please tell me on what errand you go.'

'I will tell you,' she replied softly. 'My chief reason was to find you.'

Pwyll was amazed. 'I am glad to hear it but will you now tell me who you are?'

'My name is Rhiannon, the daughter of Heveydd Hen. A marriage has been arranged for me but I do not like the man. I love you and you only, and I have come here to ask if you could love me, too.'

'By heaven,' cried Pwyll, 'if I could choose any lady in the world, I would choose you.'

'Promise to meet me then before I am given to another.'

'That I will gladly do,' said Pwyll.

'Meet me then in a year's time at the place of Heveydd,' said Rhiannon.

Pwyll agreed to this and they parted. In a year's time the Prince took one hundred knights with him and went to the palace of Heveydd Hen, where he was made very welcome. When they sat down to a feast in the great hall of the palace, Rhiannon's father sat on one side of Pwyll and Rhiannon herself on the other. After they had eaten, a tall auburn-haired youth entered and was made welcome by Pwyll and his companions.

'I come as a suitor,' said the young man, 'and would ask a favour of you.'

'Whatever you ask shall be granted,' said Pwyll, at which Rhiannon cried out, 'Why did you say that, my Lord? Why?'

'The lady whom I love,' said the youth, 'is to be your bride tonight. I ask that you give her to me.'

Pwyll, horrified, was silent.

'Be silent then,' said Rhiannon, 'for you have made a foolish promise. This man who asks for me is the one my father had chosen and whom I do not want. His name is Gwawl, a man of great power and wealth. Now you must keep your promise for you are a man of honour.'

At last Pwyll spoke. 'Lady, I cannot lose you but I must not bring shame to my people. What am I to do?'

'Give me to him,' said Rhiannon, 'and I shall see to it that I can never be truly his. Take this sack, look after it well. I will consent to be the bride of Gwawl at the end of the year. Come here for the wedding celebrations and bring the sack with you; also bring your knights and let them hide in the orchard. When we are in the middle of joy and feasting, come into the hall dressed as a beggar and I will put a spell on the sack so that, however much is placed in it, it will never be full. Gwawl will ask whether the sack could ever be full . . .' and Rhiannon gave Pwyll more instructions as to what else he should do when the time came.

Gwawl went back to his lands and Pwyll returned to Dyfed. At the end of the year, they both came to Heveydd Hen for the marriage celebrations, Pwyll putting his hundred knights in the orchard as Rhiannon had instructed. When the feast was at its height, Pwyll entered the hall, wearing ragged clothes and old shoes upon his feet, with the sack clutched in one hand.

'Greetings to this beggar,' said Gwawl, not recognising Pwyll in this disguise. 'And what do you require of us?'

'Meat enough, my lord, to fill this sack,' replied Pwyll.

'An easy request to grant,' said Gwawl, and he ordered his servants to fill the sack but, though they put more and more food into it, still the sack was no fuller than before.

'Will the sack never be filled?' asked Pwyll.

'It will not,' replied Gwawl, 'until one who is powerful and wealthy shall tread down with his feet the food in the sack.'

'Rise up, Gwawl,' encouraged Rhiannon. 'Only you can do this thing.'

So Gwawl rose from the table and put his two feet in the sack and Pwyll turned up the sides, shut up the sack and tied it at the top, with Gwawl inside. Then he blew his horn and his men came from the orchard into the hall and set upon Gwawl's men. And, as each of Pwyll's knights came into the hall, he struck the sack so that Gwawl cried out, 'Listen to me; I have no wish to be slain in a sack.'

Heveydd, Rhiannon's father, intervened and said he thought Gwawl had had more punishment than he deserved.

'What shall I do now?' Pwyll asked Rhiannon, whose scheme so far had worked so well.

'You are now in a position,' she said, 'to get a pledge from him that he will not seek revenge and that I may be your bride and not the bride of Gwawl.'

'I will do this gladly,' said Gwawl when he heard Rhiannon speak, and he was instantly released and so were those of his knights who had been taken prisoner.

'I am hurt and have many bruises,' said Gwawl to Pwyll, 'and should like to return to my own country.'

'This you may do,' said Pwyll, 'while I stay here for my marriage celebrations.'

Pwyll and Rhiannon were married and that night was spent in feasting and merry-making. The next day husband and wife set off for Narberth where there was more feasting, and many noblemen and noble ladies came to greet the new bride and each was given a gift from Rhiannon, sometimes a bracelet or a ring or a precious stone. And she and Pwyll reigned happily over the land of Dyfed for many years.

It is said that Rhiannon brought with her to her husband her marvellous birds who sang only on rare occasions but whose song when heard made warriors spellbound for eighty years.

'Three things that are often heard,' says a Welsh triad, 'the song of the birds of Rhiannon, a song of wisom from the mouth of a Saxon, and an invitation to a feast from a miser.'

The Kidnap

Rhiannon and Pwyll had been married for three years and had no children. This worried the nobles of the land as they badly wanted Pwyll to have an heir. They came before their lord and one of them said, 'We know you are not as young as many of us and we are afraid that you may not have a son. Should you not put Rhiannon aside and take another wife?'

Pwyll was horrified by this idea as he loved Rhiannon very much. On the other hand, he understood the concern of the nobles.

'Give me one more year,' he said, 'and if there is no child by then I will do as you wish.'

Before the end of the year a son was born and six women were appointed to watch over mother and child. Rhiannon was sleeping and the women should have stayed awake but they, too, went to sleep. At break of day they awoke and to their horror, the baby was no longer in his cot.

'Alas,' cried one of the women, 'the baby is lost and we may well be put to death for our neglect of him. Is there nothing we can do in this matter?'

'Yes, there is,' said another of the women. 'There is here a hound with puppies; let us kill some of these and rub the blood on the face and hands of Rhiannon. Then we can say she had devoured her own son and six of us will be witness to this.'

And, having carried out their evil deed, they awoke Rhiannon.

'Where is my lovely baby?' asked Rhiannon sleepily.

'Lady, please do not ask us about your son,' said one of the women. 'We have blows and bruises from struggling with you and, indeed, we have never seen a woman so violent. Do you not realise you have devoured your own son?'

'For pity's sake,' cried Rhiannon, 'you lie. Please do not lie to me. Tell me the truth and I will forgive you.'

'We have told the truth,' insisted the women. And, in spite of Rhiannon's tears and pleas, they stuck by their story.

Soon the news reached the ears of Pwyll and the story spread throughout the land. The nobles came to Pwyll, begging him to put aside the wife who had committed such a dreadful crime.

'I said I would put her aside if she did not bear me a son. But this she has done and I have no cause to do this. If she has done wrong, then let her do penance for it.'

Rhiannon no longer had the strength to defend herself against the six women, so she sent for a wise man to give her a penance. The punishment imposed upon her was that she should remain in the palace of Narberth for seven years and, during that time, she should sit by a horse block that was near the gate. There she was to tell the story about her baby son to all who came and that she should offer to carry them upon her back into the palace. Fortunately, few people permitted her to do this.

Now, at this time, there lived a man called Teirnyon who was lord of Gwent is Coed, and he was a fine and good man. He owned the most beautiful mare in the kingdom and, on the night of every first day of May, this mare foaled but no one ever saw the colt. It just disappeared.

One night Teirnyon was discussing this with his wife. 'I cannot understand,' he said, 'how it is we never see any of the colts and, as this is the night of the first of May, I am determined to find out what happens.'

He armed himself and went to the stable and stayed there until, as darkness fell, the mare gave birth to a beautiful foal. When Teirnyon came nearer to it, he heard a great noise and, after the noise, a huge claw came through the table window and seized the colt by the mane. Teirnyon drew his sword and struck off the arm of this dreadful beast. The noise was followed by a sound of wailing and Teirnyon opened the stable door and rushed out into the darkness to discover what or who was causing such a disturbance. It was too dark for him to see anything so he returned to the house where, on the front doorstep, he found a baby boy wrapped in white satin.

He took the baby into the bedroom where his wife was sleeping.

'Lady, are you asleep?' asked Teirnyon.

'Indeed I was, my lord, but now you have awakened me.'

'I have done so in good cause for I have a surprise for you, my dear. As you have never had a child, look, I bring you a baby boy.' And Teirnyon told his wife exactly what had happened.

'What kind of clothes is he dressed in?' asked his wife.

'In fine clothes of white satin,' he replied.

'Then he is a child of a good family,' said his wife, 'and I shall pretend that I have been pregnant and that the child is mine.'

Later, the child was baptized and christened Gwri Wallt Euryn because his hair was golden. He grew to be a sturdy lad and, when he was four years old, Teirnyon's wife asked her husband, 'Where is the colt you saved on the night when you found our son?'

'It has been cared for by the grooms,' came the reply.

'Then would it not be a good idea if you had the colt broken in and thus made ready to be given to the boy for riding.'

So the beautiful pony was given to the boy.

While all this was happening, news of Rhiannon and her penance reached their ears, and Teirnyon felt sorry for Rhiannon and he asked questions as to what actually happened. Then, thinking about the sad tale, he found he was looking closely at the boy. Teirnyon knew Pwyll as he had once been one of that prince's men. And the more he looked at the boy, the more he thought how the lad resembled Pwyll. He felt he had done wrong to keep the boy when he knew him to be the son of another man. He confided his worry to his wife, saying that it was not right for a good and innocent lady like Rhiannon to suffer when the boy was so obviously alive. Teirnyon's wife agreed that the boy should be sent to Pwyll, although she was sad at the thought of losing him.

'But perhaps, my lord,' she said, 'we may gain three things by this. Thanks from Rhiannon for releasing her from her punishment; thanks from Pwyll for nursing his son and restoring him to his rightful parents; and, thirdly, as he is a kind boy and loves us, he can be a good foster son to us.'

The very next day Teirnyon and the boy set off for Narberth, the boy riding the colt which had been given to him. As they drew near to the palace, they saw Rhiannon sitting beside the horse block.

'My lords,' she said, 'go no further on your horses. I will carry you into the palace as that is my punishment for devouring my own son.'

'Fair Lady,' said Teirnyon, 'I shall not consent to be carried on your back.'

'Nor, indeed, shall I,' said the boy.

So Teirnyon, the boy and Rhiannon went into the Palace where Pwyll greeted them and, over dinner, Teirnyon told them about the adventure of the mare and the arrival of the baby boy.

'Behold, here is your son,' said Teirnyon. 'He is so like you, his father, my lord Pwyll, that no-one can doubt he is your son.'

Rhiannon warmly embraced the boy, saying, 'Now all my troubles are over.'

'Lady,' said Teirnyon, 'we have called the boy Gwri Wallt Euryn because of the colour of his hair, but I expect you had already named him.'

'He was called Pryderi,' said Rhiannon.

'And it is only right,' said Pwyll, 'that he be called the name his mother gave him when he was born. Heaven reward you Teirnyon for you have brought up the boy well and it is fitting that he should repay you for your care.'

'My lord,' said Teirnyon, 'it was my wife who nursed him and she is sad to part from him.'

'While I live,' said Pwyll, 'I shall support you and your good wife and the boy shall always regard you with affection as his foster parents.'

Teirnyon was then offered precious jewels, fine horses and well-trained dogs but he refused them all.

Pryderi, the son of Pwyll and Rhiannon, grew up to be a fine young man, skilled in arms and sport, and, when his father died, he took his place and ruled wisely and well over Dyfed, being much loved by all his subjects.

Rhys ap Thomas

Chief among the Welshmen who helped to put on the throne Henry Tudor was Rhys ap Thomas, a great lord of south west Wales and a man who had in his veins the blood of ancient Welsh princes. When Richard III was king, Rhys pretended allegiance to him.

'Your Majesty, the man you fear, Henry Tudor, Henry of Richmond, will advance only over my body,' assured Rhys.

The King accepted this assurance not guessing that, though Rhys would not lie to him, he was a cunning man.

Henry landed with his forces at Dale, a secluded bay near Milford Haven. It was a Sunday evening and Rhys ap Thomas was there to greet the man who was to become the first Welsh king of England. Henry saw Rhys approach, riding his famous horse, Llwyd y Bacse, and surrounded by his men. Rhys dismounted and Henry greeted him warmly, encouraged by the sight of so many Welshmen eager to help him.

'My lord,' said Rhys, 'I made a promise to King Richard.'

'A promise to that tyrant,' retorted Henry, wondering if this man was, in fact, an ally. 'What did you promise?'

'I swore that you would advance to London only over my body.'

Henry Tudor frowned. 'You mean you have no intention of helping me to victory?'

'No, that's not what I mean,' and to the astonishment of the crowd Rhys lay down on the ground.

'What are you doing, man?' Henry demanded to know. 'Get up at once.'

'Not until you have stepped over me,' grinned Rhys, and Henry and the company of men began to laugh. Henry moved towards Rhys's body and, with dignity, stepped over it. More laughter ensued before the plans for victory were discussed seriously.

Henry had already written to many Welsh lords, asking for their support and they did not let him down. 'Father Rhys,' as Henry was to call him, had seen to it that, for once, the Welsh princes would cease quarrelling among themselves. Some time before Henry's invasion, he had made famous his home, Carew Castle, by inviting to a great tournament the elite of Wales and,

Rhys ap Thomas

to everyone's surprise, they all accepted – Perotts, Wogans, Herberts, Morgans, Butlers, Vaughans and Mansells among them. Rhys was Governor of Wales and probably the wealthiest and greatest person in that country. The entertainment at Carew was lavish and lasted a week. And, due to Rhys's wisdom and influence, no sword was drawn in anger nor a cross word spoken. On the first day of the great festival, Rhys led his glittering throng, with drums beating and trumpets blowing, to hear mass from the Bishop of St. David's. His guests, brought together in peace for the first time, were among the many Welshmen who helped Henry Tudor to victory.

At the head of a considerable force, Rhys ap Thomas led his men through mid-Wales. 'A worthy sight it was to see,' went an old ballad, 'how the Welshmen rose wholly with Henry, and shogged them to Shrewsbury.'

From Shrewsbury, they marched on to Stafford and, finally to the battlefield of Bosworth where they joined with Henry's English supporters and Richard III was beaten and deposed. The new king had a Welshman's love of music and encouraged poets and bards. He took pains to stress his connection with Wales. His eldest son was christened Arthur, after the legendary king, and Henry employed heralds to trace his Welsh ancestry. He amply rewarded Rhys ap Thomas, making him virtual ruler of South Wales.

William de Braose

Rhys ap Thomas was a man much loved and respected but the Normans William de Braose was neither loved nor respected. He was the ogre of the Welsh borderland in the 12th century and had a continual battle with the Welsh who, it has to be admitted, had killed his uncle, the Bishop of Hereford.

William de Braose committed one dastardly crime that roused the country. He was the ruling power in that part of Wales now called Breconshire and, being annoyed by Vaughan of Brecon, he sent a seemingly friendly invitation for Vaughan to meet him in the town. Vaughan was honoured to be asked by this powerful lord and eagerly greeted him, putting an arm on his shoulder when William called out to his men. 'Seize this man, tie him to his horse's tail.' He was instantly obeyed and the ill-fated Vaughan was dragged through the town while the townsfolk looked on in horror.

'I beg for mercy, Lord de Braose,' murmured the exhausted man when the horse finally came to a standstill.

'I do not recognise the word mercy,' replied William coldly, and immediately ordered his execution.

Powysland was still under its native princes and the one at this time was Gwenwynyn, a relative of the ill-fated Vaughan.

'I shall sweep the country of de Braose bare as a board,' he boasted, and then marched in force and laid seige to Pain-castle where de Braose awaited him. The rage of the Powys prince pitted itself in vain against the Norman's fortress.

Perhaps the foulest of de Braose's deeds was the slaughter of a roomful of Welsh guests at his own table. He had invited a large party at Christmas. The festivities were at their height when William called for silence.

'I have a demand to make,' William shouted. 'In future I expect everyone here to take an oath not to carry arms when going about your daily business.'

A ripple of discontent ran through the hall. Then all was silent until one man rose to his feet and spoke out.

'My lord, William de Braose, this is an impossible oath for any one of us to make. These are troubled times; men need to be armed to protect themselves. I beg of you to reconsider your demand.'

William frowned. 'Are there others here who resent my request?'

There came a chorus of 'Ayes' and nodding of many heads with more murmurs of resentment.

This was, in fact, exactly what William had expected and gave him an excuse, if excuse was needed, to shout for the doors of the hall to be opened. De Braose's soldiers were waiting for the order and they now poured into the hall, killing every Welshman who was present. Later on, the sons and nephews of the murdered men rose and attacked William's fortress in Breconshire. Unfortunately, with his usual good luck, the wretched tyrant was not there at the time and escaped retribution.

De Braose did not quarrel only with Welshmen; he also had a squabble with King John himself, which was aggravated by William's wife Maude, herself a difficult and truculent lady. John hated her as she refused his demand to give up her sons as hostages for her husband's good behaviour.

'Your Majesty,' said Maude, 'my sons stay in Wales with my husband who is loyal to you and always has been.'

'That's as may be,' replied the King, 'but he stirs up trouble wherever he goes. If you refuse to let me have your sons, you may well be very sorry.'

Maude was firm and proud. Maybe she thought her husband would come to the rescue. At any rate, John had her imprisoned together with one son who happened to be in London with her and there, at Windsor, they eventually died.

Another son, sickened perhaps by his father's brutality, turned to religion and not only did he become Bishop of Hereford like his great-uncle, but he also succeeded to his father's estates in Brecon and Abergavenny. But he did not live long to enjoy his position and a third brother succeeded and married a daughter of the Welsh prince Llewellyn the Great. He was the last of the de Braoses whose name had been so feared for so long.

Lake Savaddan

Three men, Welsh lords, were returning from Brecon from the court of Henry II. It was winter and the journey had been hard but it was a fine day and, when they came to Lake Savaddan, surrounded by the green heights of the Brecon Beacons, they dismounted from their horses to rest a while . It was a still windless day, not a ripple on the lake and not a sound of any sort anywhere.

The three men were Milo, Earl of Hereford and Lord of Brecon; Payn Fitz John, Lord of Ewyas; and Griffith ap Rhys who was not lord of anywhere. Now Milo and Payn possessed rich districts but young Griffith possessed nothing very much although he came from a long and noble line.

There was a flock of wild fowl on the lake which caught Milo's attention.

'Seeing those birds over there,' he said to his companions, 'I am reminded of a Welsh tradition.'

'What tradition is that?' asked Payn.

'Well, it is said that the birds of Savaddan will only sing at the command of a natural prince of our country.'

Payn laughed. 'Griffith claims to be of nobler birth than either of us, let us now see which of the three of us is prince of our country.'

'That is a somewhat foolish suggestion,' said Milo, 'but nonetheless I'll go along with it, if Griffith agrees.'

Griffith had remained silent until now. 'I certainly agree,' he said. 'I have nothing to lose. Who shall go first?'

'Milo,' said Payn, 'as he is the eldest of us.'

'If the birds are going to sing, they'll certainly sing for me,' said Milo.

The three men moved to the edge of the lake; the sun shimmered on the water and shadows of the mountains shifted to and fro.

'Birds!' cried out Milo, his voice echoing across the lake. 'I, Milo, lord of Hereford and Brecon, command you to sing and acknowledge my noble birth.'

A few birds rose into the air, flapping their wings before

77

returning to float serenely on the water. There was not a sound from them.

'Come on, birds, sing, sing!' shouted Milo impatiently. But no birds sang.

'You have failed, Milo' said Payn, 'it is obvious that the birds have no intention of obeying you. It is now my turn. Griffith is the youngest, so he can go last, if it should prove necessary which I doubt.'

Griffith smiled. 'You are wasting your time, Payn; I am the only true noble of the three of us.'

Milo and Payn laughed scornfully. 'You own nothing,' said Milo.

'It is nobility of birth which is at stake here,' said Griffith, 'not possession of lands. But, come along, Payn, issue your command if you will.'

Payn moved even nearer to the lake, his boots touching the edge of the water.

'Birds!' he cried out in a loud voice, 'I, Payn Fitz John, Lord of Ewyas, command you to sing and acknowledge my noble birth.'

Again, a few birds flapped their wings and a couple skimmed away into the distance. There was not a sound from them.

'Birds,' shouted Payn in an even louder voice. 'Sing, I command you to sing.' But no birds sang.

It was Griffith's turn to laugh. 'Both of you have failed,' he said, 'now we shall see if the birds will sing for me.'

'It's only a superstition,' muttered Milo, 'the birds will sing for no-one; after all, water birds make odd quacking noises; they do not really *sing* at all.'

'Let us mount our horses and continue our journey,' said Payn. 'Enough of this nonsense.'

'It is only fair that I should have my turn,' insisted Griffith and, after a short argument, Milo and Payn agreed.

To the astonishment of his friends, Griffith went down on his knees and began to pray as he would do on the eve of a battle. His prayer finished, he fixed his eyes on the flock of birds and, fairly quietly, he spoke to them.

Lake Savaddan

'Birds,' he said, 'I, Griffith ap Rhys, a nobleman without possessions, command you to sing and acknowledge my noble birth.'

Milo and Payn were already mounting their horses when the birds all rose together, beating the water with their wings, and a chorus of the sweetest bird song filled the air.

'There, listen to that,' said Griffith triumphantly. 'Perhaps now you will acknowledge that I am indeed a prince of the land.'

Milo and Payn were too amazed at the sight and sound of the birds that they could only nod their heads. Griffith had won the day.

The Kidnapping of St. Patrick

Although St. Patrick is the patron saint of Ireland, he was, in fact, a Welshman, born in a small village in Glamorgan. His original Welsh name was Pedrawg which became altered to Pedrig and Patric and, finally to Patrick. When he was sixteen years old, Irish pirates descended on the village and Patrick was kidnapped and taken to Ireland where, for six years, he was slave to an Irishman called Milcho, his main job being to feed the cattle.

When he was 22 years of age, he had a vivid dream in which he heard a voice saying, 'Patrick, you shall return quickly to your own country,' and then, after a while, the voice spoke again, 'Lo, the ship is ready.' Encouraged by this dream, Patrick ran away from Milcho and, after a long and exhausting journey of about 200 miles, he came to the coast and there, in the harbour, he saw a ship that was about to sail for Wales.

'I should dearly like to go home to Wales,' Patrick told the skipper of the ship, 'but, alas, I have no money to pay for my passage. Perhaps you could take me on as one of the crew.'

'I do not need more hands on board,' replied the skipper, 'and, if you cannot pay, I am not prepared to take you as a passenger.'

So Patrick, disheartened, returned to a small hut nearby where he had stayed the previous night. There, he went down on his knees and began to pray for help. As he was praying, he heard one of the sailors shouting to him. 'Come quickly, the skipper has changed his mind.' Patrick hurried to the quayside where the skipper said to him, 'I cannot say why I have suddenly decided to take you with us but you can be one of us and we will receive you, trusting in your good faith.'

The ship sailed for three days before land was sighted. Suddenly a great wind blew up, the sea boiled and flung huge waves over the tiny ship which was driven relentlessly on to some cruel rocks where it was smashed to pieces. Fortunately and miraculously none of the crew was drowned and they all managed to struggle ashore. There were no houses to be seen and no sign of any activity so the men began to walk inland in the hope of finding help. For twenty eight days they tramped on, without food or water until the skipper, in desperation, spoke to Patrick and begged for his help.

'You are a Christian,' he said, 'your God is great and powerful. Will you not pray for us as we are in danger of dying from hunger?'

Patrick went down on his knees and began to pray. He had not been praying for long when a herd of swine appeared which the crew immediately killed, made a fire and cooked and ate the roasted meat. Thus refreshed, they continued on their way, now regarding Patrick as a symbol of good luck and his god as very powerful. After many weeks, Patrick reached his home near Cowbridge and bade his companions farewell.

Twice again, poor Patrick was kidnapped by Irish pirates but, each time he managed to escape and return home. Then, one day, he had another important dream in which he heard Irish voices saying, 'We beg you, holy youth, to come again to us and teach us about your God.'

Patrick's parents beseeched their son not to leave home yet again; they found it difficult to understand why Patrick should wish to return to a country where he had been treated so badly and whose people appeared to be barbarians. But Patrick was determined. He left his native village, stopping a while at St. David's where he built a monastery to the glory of God. He was very happy there and would have stayed but he had a vision in which an angel commanded him to leave Wales and go to Ireland. Reluctantly, he did this and stayed there, teaching Christianity to the Irish heathens and finally dying far away from his beloved Wales.

Gruffydd, Son of Cynan

In the days when William Rufus was king of England, there lived two Welshmen, close friends, called Gruffydd, son of Cynan and Rhys, son of Tudor. They met in Ireland where they were both exiles from Wales, having been beaten in battle by warring chieftains. Together, they plotted and planned their return to Wales to regain the lands they had lost. It was arranged that Rhys should return first to West Wales and that, later, Gruffydd should join him with an army of Irish soldiers. They finally met up to fight the usurper of North Wales, a chieftain called Trehaiarn. A great battle ensued in the county of Montgomery at a place called Carno Mount. Trehaiarn and his army were routed and Gruffydd and his troops went in pursuit of the fleeing enemy. But, for some reason, Rhys and his men departed for the south, without leaving a word of explanation. There, in Glamorgan, they continued to fight but this time the enemy was another chieftain.

Now, when Gruffydd discovered that Rhys had departed after the great battle with Trehaiarn he was greatly offended and, while Rhys was in Glamorgan, Gruffydd ravaged Rhys's lands which were in West Wales. Soon Gruffydd found himself sandwiched between the warriors of Powys and the army of Rhys who had quickly left the south to defend his own lands. Gruffydd managed to give them both the slip and returned to North Wales where he was soon crowned king. But the Earl of Chester and the Earl of Shrewsbury considered he had behaved badly towards his former friend Rhys and they sent a man to tell Gruffydd that they wanted a private interview with him. Innocently, Gruffydd went to the meeting place with only a few of his soldiers. He was instantly taken prisoner and imprisoned in Chester Castle.

He was a prisoner for twelve long years before he was rescued by one, Cynfrig Hir, or 'the Tall'. One night horses were placed somewhere in the suburbs of Chester; in charge of them were some of Cynfrig's daring companions, there being one extra horse in the hope that Gruffydd would be freed to ride it.

Cynfrig crept into the castle where Gruffydd was in close

fetters in the dungeon so it had not seemed necessary to guard him closely. With one blow, Cynfrig felled the one guard who was on duty, grabbing from him the keys to the dungeons. Inside one of these, on the rough floor, sat the one-time king.

'Quick, my lord, there is little time to waste,' said Cynfrig.

'Alas, I am too weak to walk,' groaned Gruffydd, trying in vain to struggle to his feet.

'Get on my back then,' urged the tall Cynfrig, 'I'm strong and will try to carry you.'

'And what of my fetters?' asked Gruffydd.

'No time to remove those now and, anyway, I have nothing with me to shatter them.'

Painfully, Gruffydd tried again to get to his feet and, this time, he managed to stand without falling. Soon he was on the brave man's big and broad back, and Cynfrig ran as fast as he could through the many corridors of the castle. There was the sound of merriment in the great hall. The Earl of Chester was entertaining and a great number of his men were with him so that the rest of the castle was mainly deserted. Across the drawbridge hurried Cynfrig and the burden on his back, and he had joined his followers before the alarm had been sounded. With the fettered king in their midst, the Welshmen leapt on to their sturdy Welsh ponies and they were away from Chester and heading into their own country. They galloped to Cynfrig's straw-thatched cottage with its white-washed walls.

'It is but a humble abode, my lord, but at least you will be safe here,' said Cynfrig.

'It is a palace in my eyes,' said Gruffydd, 'and I am greatly indebted to you.'

Inside the cottage were hammers and chisels and it was not long before Gruffydd was freed from his Norman chains. The king stayed there, near Bala, until he was strong enough to make another journey. Cynfrig conveyed his Majesty to Anglesey and then he made his way to his royal relatives in Ireland. It was not long before he had mustered another army and returned to North Wales where he found the Normans had made themselves masters. With his warring spirit now revived, Gruffydd and his warriors were soon fighting and burning and knocking down the buildings of the foreigners. His former captors, the Earls of Chester and Shrewsbury now marched against him and he only narrowly escaped being made their prisoner yet again.

He managed to reach the sanctuary of a monastery of Aberdaron where one of the monks wrote down a description of the king of North Wales. 'He was a man of medium height. His hair was golden, his face round and of a healthy hue. His eyes were large and handsome and he had fine eyebrows. His beard, like his hair, was fair, and the latter was cropped round. His skin was fair, his limbs strong and athletic. His fingers were long and his feet shapely. He was a master of languages and spoke with eloquence. He was of a stately presence. He was merciful to his friends, but cruel to his foes.'

The monks of Aberdaron lent him the small boat they used for travelling to and from Bardsey Island. In this small craft, the exhausted Gruffydd reached Ireland once more in safety.

Gruffydd was not a man to give in easily and, once again, he returned to fight in North Wales. He endured great hardships, sleeping in caves, trudging on foot, often thirsty and hungry. Still he did not succeed in regaining his lands and, this time, he and the nine men who were left with him, had to turn their faces yet again to Ireland. They found a boat which they hoped would take them there but, unfortunately, it was driven up the Bristol Channel and came, not to Ireland, but to Llantwit Major in Glamorgan. Irish pirates, like those who kidnapped St. Patrick, frequently landed on this part of the coast and Gruffydd and his men were suspected, by the local population, of being some of these pirates. More fighting ensued and ceased only when Gruffydd managed to persuade his South Wales enemies that he was indeed the king of North Wales.

After many further struggles with his old enemies of Chester and Shrewsbury, Gruffydd was finally recognised as the King of North Wales by Henry I of England, brother of William Rufus whom he had succeeded. Gruffydd, son of Cynan, was at last peacefully seated on the throne of his ancestors.

Lady Nesta Newmarch

Lady Nesta, daughter of the King Trehairn who was killed at the battle of Carno Mount, ran across the meadow towards an old oak tree, behind which, waiting for her, was her husband. Their meetings had to be secret as the young Welshman, called Hywel, was not of noble birth and consent to the marriage would never have been given by Nesta's relations. This day Nesta threw herself into her husband's arms, the tears pouring down her cheeks.

'Why do you cry so, my love?' asked Hywel. 'There should only be smiles on your lovely face with the joy of our meeting.'

'I have good cause for tears,' replied Nesta. 'Alas, I know not what to do. I am being pressed to marry a Norman lord called Bernard Newmarch and I think I shall have to do so. I fear for your life should it be discovered that you and I are married.'

For a few moments, Hywel said nothing, then he spoke quietly and sadly. 'It must be as you say. Our happiness has been for only so short a time but I'll not stand in your way. Go ahead with the wedding; at least there will be more ceremony than ever you and I had.'

Still weeping, Nesta put her arms round her husband's neck. 'Farewell then, sweetheart; I shall always love you and I shall never forget you.' And, turning away from him, she ran back across the meadow, turning only once to take a last look at the man she loved. Not wishing to cause him any further worry, she had not told Hywel that she was expecting his child.

Hywel disappeared from the area and joined the army, believing it best to go as far away as possible from the Lady Nesta.

Nesta's marriage to Lord Bernard Newmarch went ahead and, some months later, she bore Hywel's son. Lord Newmarch naturally assumed the boy was his. Lady Newmarch, being consumed with guilt, went to confess to the Prior of Brecon.

'I bear a great burden,' she confessed. 'I am married to a poor Welsh knight but have kept this marriage secret. He has gone away and I am illegally married to Lord Bernard Newmarch.

I have given birth to a son but the father is my true husband and not Lord Newmarch. I trust this secret is safe with you and that I may some time be forgiven for loving too much and behaving so badly.'

The Prior assured her he would say nothing about what he had heard, and Nesta left the Priory, happier now that she had confessed her sins.

The baby son was christened Mahel and a girl child, born a few years later, was christened Sybil. Mahel, not knowing anything about his real Welsh father, grew up to manhood believing himself to be a Norman like the man he assumed was his father, and to be Welsh by his mother. It was to the Norman's advantage to marry Welsh ladies of noble birth, they bringing much land as dowry and sometimes the hope of peace.

Lord Newmarch died soon after Mahel's twentieth birthday and it was then that a stranger of military appearance presented himself at Brecon Priory. The arrival of this poor Welshman was greeted with no surprise by the Prior, who had kept the secret entrusted to him by Nesta. The stranger, of course, was Nesta's long lost husband. The Prior hurried to the castle.

'Lady Nesta, I have great news for you,' said the Prior.

Nesta did not look up from her embroidery. Any small item of gossip was great news to the Prior.

'You must prepare yourself for a shock, my lady,' the Prior went on.

At these words, Nesta raised her eyes to him. 'It is not bad news about my son or daughter, is it?' she asked anxiously.

'No, my lady. A stranger came to the Priory this morning. Can you guess who it was?'

'Do not play games with me,' said Nesta coldly.

'He is none other than your true husband,' said the Prior triumphantly.

Nesta dropped her embroidery and rose to her feet.

'You are not teasing me,' she cried. 'Tell me you are not teasing. It is truly Hywel, my beloved husband?'

'It surely is that very man, returned from fighting abroad. He came here as soon as he learnt you were a widow.'

'This is wonderful news you bring to me, good Prior. Please

bring my husband here in an hour or so when I shall be prepared to meet him.'

Hywel was grey-haired and he stooped a little. Nesta's hair was still the colour of chestnuts, with just a few flecks of grey, and she stood erect in front of her husband, who scarcely noticed the lines on her face. Their reunion was tender and tearful. It was as if they had never been parted. But living together openly as husband and wife was still impossible now that Nesta was Lady Newmarch and Hywel was still only a poor Welsh knight. However, arrangements were made for the couple to meet regularly and, though their meetings were supposed to be secret, it was not long before Nesta's son Mahel observed the stranger's comings and goings. He was greatly annoyed by what he considered impertinence on the part of this stranger. His attentions should not be encouraged by Mahel's widowed mother. Mahel planned to waylay this unwelcome visitor and put an end to the matter.

One moonlit night, Hywel had left the castle and was on his way back to the Priory where he now lived, when Mahel leapt out at him from behind a hawthorn hedge. Now, although Mahel did not know Hywel was his real father, Nesta had told her husband that Mahel was his son. Hywel immediately recognised the boy. Mahel drew his sword and waited for Hywel to draw his. Mahel was no great fighter but his father was an experienced swordsman. However, Hywel had no wish to fight or harm his son so he merely parried the young man's sword thrusts and put up practically no opposition. It was not long before Mahel struck his father a fatal blow.

When Nesta heard the dreadful news of Hywel's death and by whose hand he had died, she was frantic with grief and anger. She vowed she would never again see Mahel.

Soon after this tragic affair, Henry I of England came to Worcester to receive the homage of borderland lords. Nesta was there in her capacity as the Lady of Brecon and, after she had curtseyed to the king, she asked if she might speak a few words of great importance.

'It shall be as you wish,' said Henry, 'and we shall gladly listen to words from the mouth of so beautiful a lady.'

Nesta was pale but composed. 'What I have to say may not

be welcome to your ears, your Majesty.'

'Nevertheless, speak on,' said the king.

'My husband, the Late Bernard Newmarch, was not the father of my son Mahel.'

A stunned silence followed this astonishing statement. Then the king spoke gently to Nesta. 'Perhaps, Lady Nesta, you do not know what you are saying. Maybe you have a fever.'

'I know full well what I am saying and, thank you, your Majesty, but I am in command of all my senses. I was never the legal wife of Lord Bernard. I had been married before and Mahel is my son by Hywel, a soldier now dead.'

Still, Henry could not believe what he was hearing and he demanded that the holy relics of the Cathedral of Worcester be brought before him. Nesta was commanded to swear on these that what she had said was true. This Nesta did, repeating everything she had previously said, confessing her sinful secret yet again.

Thus was Nesta revenged on Mahel for the death of Hywel. Mahel was immediately disinherited. But Sybil, who was also illegitimate in that Nesta was not legally married to her father Lord Bernard, was nevertheless made an heiress and later married the Earl of Hereford who, through this marriage, became also the Earl of Brecon.

Robert Fitzhamon and the Welshman

Robert Fitzhamon, Norman lord of Cardiff Castle, set out one day into the countryside where a meet of the Fitzhamon hounds was to take place. It was a crisp autumn day and the sun shone weakly down on the group of huntsmen. In the excitement of the chase down the Glamorgan Vale, Sir Robert became isolated from the group of his Norman followers. He was riding across a field which led into a wood and, in the distance he could hear the cry of the hounds and the voices of the huntsmen urging them on. Sir Robert had spurred on his horse in his anxiety to join the band of his men when his horse stumbled, reared on its hind legs and threw his rider to the ground. He lay there, helpless, his left leg causing him great pain; there seemed little doubt that he had broken it and there was no-one near to help him. He groaned aloud and cried out for assistance. All was quiet but for the singing of the birds; even the noise of the hunt had receded into the distance. No-one heard Fitzhamon's cries and, for some minutes, he remained quietly, pondering on what he should do. He tried to get to his feet but the pain in his leg proved too much for him and he lay back again on the ground.

While he was lying helpless, there came a rustle from the nearby woods and, to Sir Robert's dismay, there appeared out of the green forest, one of the local Welsh lords whom, together with many others, Fitzhamon had deprived of his lands, giving them to the Norman lords. Instant death was what he now expected. The Welshman looked fierce and had a long knife in his hand. The Norman crossed himself and hoped he was prepared to meet his Maker. Slowly the Welshman approached, looking even more menacing as he did so. Fitzhamon prayed it would all be over quickly. He could expect no mercy from any Welshman. Then, to his amazement, the Welshman placed his knife into his belt and bent over the Norman lord.

'You are injured,' he said. Fitzhamon nodded and wished again that he might be killed quickly. The Welshman ran his hand down the injured leg. Fitzhamon winced.

'Your leg is broken,' said the Welshman. Sir Robert nodded

again. He began to be more hopeful; perhaps, after all, this man was not going to kill him. The Welshman turned away and began to walk back towards the woods.

'Do not leave me here,' begged Fitzhamon but the Welshman did not reply. Sir Robert now came to the conclusion that he was being left to die with no-one to aid him but then the Welshman re-appeared with a stripped branch of tree and preceded to strap Fitzhamon's injured leg to the makeshift splint. He was, like many Welshmen, small, dark and stocky, a much smaller man than Sir Robert but nevertheless he lifted the Norman lord up from the ground and put him on his horse who had been quietly cropping the grass at his master's feet. Not only was his leg injured but Fitzhamon was badly bruised and shaken and so shocked that he did not object when the Welshman led him to a willow cabin where he lived in the depth of the woods. There he tenderly lifted Sir Robert off the horse and laid him down on a bed of bracken.

Sir Robert stayed there, carefully nursed and fed by the Welshman until he was fit enough to be moved. When the day came for him to go back to Cardiff Castle, he mounted his horse and looked down at his benefactor.

'Look after that leg now,' said the Welshman, 'and take no strenuous exercise until it is quite recovered.'

Fitzhamon smiled at him but the Welshman did not smile back.

'Something has puzzled me,' said Sir Robert, 'may I ask you a question?'

'Certainly,' said the Welshman, refusing to call any Norman 'My lord.'

'Why, when I have done you and your countrymen so much harm, did you not kill me when you had the chance?'

Now the Welshman did smile. 'I found you defenceless on the ground and no Welshman ever strikes a man when he is down. I doubt if you Normans behave in so honourable a fashion.'

Sir Robert ignored the jibe. He was a relative of William the Conqueror and a powerful man. He looked at this poor Welsh lord who had probably saved his life and spoke out in the voice of authority.

'In gratitude for your help in my predicament, I here and now order that all your land and possessions which we have stolen from you shall be returned to you immediately.'

When he arrived back at the Castle, Fitzhamon not only saw to it that this particular Welshman should have his land restored to him but he set about doing the same for many other Welsh landlords of Glamorgan.

A few miles to the west of Cardiff there is to this day a hill called 'Tumbledown Dick', a curious name which possibly marks the spot where, so many hundreds of years ago, a Norman lord broke his leg and was found there by a Welsh lord.

Gwilym Jones of Newland

Gwilym and his parents lived in the village of Newland near the town of Monmouth. He was a bright, lively boy and, when he was old enough to work, he asked his father if he might apply for a job in the town.

'They want a boy to help with the chores of the King's Head Inn,' he said. 'Do you think, father, that I might get the job?'

His father was delighted to know the boy might be working as they were a poor family and extra money was always welcome. He gladly encouraged the boy to apply for the job and this Gwilym did, and obtained the post.

Now some years later there came a young lady to help the innkeeper. She was a handsome woman, a cousin of the innkeeper, well-educated and full of charm. It was not long before Gwilym had fallen in love with her but she was a lady and he only a kitchen boy. However, as the girl was always sweet and pleasant to him, he decided he could lose nothing if he proposed to her. He was alone in the kitchen, peeling potatoes, when she came to ask if the meal was nearly ready.

'It won't be long, madam,' was the reply, 'and, while we are alone, I have something I should like to ask you.'

The lady was surprised at the serious manner of the scullion. She nodded her lovely head and Gwilym put down the knife he had been using and faced her.

'You are the most beautiful maiden I have ever seen and the sweetest; I should be honoured if you would consent to be my wife.' The words rushed out of his mouth almost before he had time to think. He was indeed a foolish lad if he thought this superior creature could ever agree to marry him. In fact, she began to laugh and her laughter hurt Gwilym more than a straight refusal would have done.

'Oh dear,' cried his lady love, 'you must be joking, Gwilym, indeed you must be joking. *Me* marry *you!* Why, I could have my pick of the finest gentlemen in Monmouth.' And, once again, she burst out laughing before hurrying from the kitchen.

Poor Gwilym was heartbroken. He realised he had been foolish but still he could not help loving this beautiful woman.

He was in a hopeless situation and, unable to bear the sight of his loved one, he decided it would be better if he left the inn and never saw her again. But, before he went, knowing he might need to walk some distance before getting another job, he went to the shoemaker, a Mr. Joe King, to buy a pair of shoes. Saying he would pay for them later, he took the shoes and ran away from the inn and Monmouth.

There were many of the shoemaker's friends who accused Gwilym of being a rogue to leave the town without paying for his shoes but Joe King was not so upset.

'Gwilym Jones is a good lad; he'll pay me whenever he can,' he said.

The years went by, rolling one after the other. Whenever his name was mentioned, it was 'that wretched young man who ran away without paying Mr. King for his shoes.' Still the kindly shoemaker said, 'Gwilym is a good young man and will pay me when he can.'

After a while, even the shoes and Gwilym Jones were forgotten.

The young saplings planted by old Mr. and Mrs. Jones were now grown into trees in the garden of the little cottage at Newland. It was a fine spring morning and the daffodils and primroses were all in flower when an elderly man in a ragged coat, his back bent like a bow, crept through the village to the cottage where he sat down on the grass under the shadow of the trees. The woman who now lived in the cottage came out of the front door and saw the stranger in her garden.

'Good day to you, ma'am,' said Gwilym, for he it was. 'May I stay here a while and beg a drink of you from the well?'

'Certainly you may not,' snapped the woman. 'This is not a place for tramps and vagabonds. Go and get some water in another place.'

'I am tired,' said Gwilym. 'I have come a long way.'

'That's of no concern to me,' said the woman. 'Go along with you, get away from my cottage and my garden or I'll set the dog on you.' Behind her was a large dog, growling and showing his teeth. Gwilym quickly rose up and made his way to the nearest alehouse in Newland where he sat down on a bench outside. The innkeeper came out and asked him what

Gwilym Jones of Newland

he wished to order. Gwilym shook his head and, 'I'd like a glass of water,' he said, 'I have no money for beer.' The innkeeper frowned.

'Go away,' he said, 'off to the poorhouse with you. Do not sit here, taking up the room of a good customer.'

So off to the poorhouse went Gwilym, who had been away for thirty years. It seemed he had returned ragged and penniless and he tried to claim relief from the parish where his mother and father had lived all their lives.

'You have been too long away,' he was told, 'and, anyway, you left Newland once to work in Monmouth. There is nothing here for you.'

'I beg for your help,' pleaded Gwilym, 'all I want is a little food and drink and somewhere to lay my head. I'm an old man and I should like to end my days here and be buried in the grave where my parents lie.'

But no pity was shown him and he was sent, hungry and footsore, on his way to Monmouth. There, he was admitted into the poorhouse and made welcome. He lived there for a time and was loved and respected by all the paupers who surrounded him. He had not been there long when he made his way to the shoemaker who was living in the same small house next door to the King's Head Inn where Gwilym had worked when a young man.

'Do your remember me, Joe King?' asked Gwilym.

'No matter whether I do or not,' said Joe gazing at him with short-sighted eyes. 'You look as if you could do with a bite to eat,' and he took the old man into his kitchen and gave him some bread and cheese.

'Do you not remember me?' asked Gwilym again. 'A good for nothing scamp of a lad who worked at the King's Head and who cheated you out of a pair of shoes?'

'Well, well,' said old Joe King. 'I do remember a boy called Gwilym Jones – wild Will some folks called him – but he was no scamp and would pay me yet if he could. And surely I may forgive a poor fellow the value of a pair of shoes.'

Next morning the pauper was gone and there was a great fuss and much talk that he had gone off with the workhouse clothes. But a month later, a coach drew up to the workhouse and out of it got a fine, broad-shouldered gentleman, with a back as straight as a poplar tree. He carried a bundle under his arm, asked for the master of the poorhouse and handed over some old clothes. It was, long before the news spread around the town that poor old Will Jones had really been, all along, the Gwilym Jones of the city of London, who had a right to stand up to the King himself and was a rich man indeed. From the workhouse, Gwilym drove straight to the shoemaker and it was not easy to persuade Joe King that this great gentleman was the boy from Newland who ran away from the inn and made his fortune and owed him for a pair of shoes. After a long talk, Gwilym left a purse, heavy with gold sovereigns, on the shoemaker's table.

Gwilym had intended to do more for Newland than he did for Monmouth but, such had been his treatment in that village, he left in his will almshouses and money for the comfort of the poor people of Monmouth only. However, he was too good a man to bear malice so he also left the sum of five thousand pounds to the people of Newland, hoping to teach them that charity should always be given to those who appear to need it.

Castell Coch

Castell Coch – the Red Castle – is so called because of the warm, red colour of the stone of which it is built. With its elegant turrets and small size, it looks like a fairy castle, rising from a crag, near Cardiff, and surrounded by trees and shrubs. In the very old days it was almost impregnable against enemies, and one occupant, Ivor Bach, used to boast that had he twelve hundred men he could beat the best twelve thousand in the world. For a long time he was a thorn in the flesh of the Norman lords of Cardiff Castle.

It is said that a subterranean passage leads from Castell Coch to Cardiff Castle and there are many stories about this supposed or other passages. In the time of Charles I, whose army held Cardiff Castle, Cromwell's soldiers were led through a passage by a Royalist deserter and were thus able to enter the Castle at dead of night, and take possession of it. The Royal traitor was executed by order of Cromwell who did not like treachery in the enemy camp any more than he did in his own.

One legend connected with Castell Coch concerns a lady who, some years ago, was allowed to rent a few rooms in the Castle, and there she lived with her old servants, a man and his wife. She heard at different times strange noises which she put down to either rats or jackdaws. One night, however, she awoke suddenly and saw, at the foot of her bed, the figure of a man dressed in the time of Charles I. How dare a man invade the privacy of her bedroom was her first thought, but he looked fixedly at her, and she was too frightened to call out. The stranger was pale and his eyes full of sorrow. The lady tried to scream but no noise came from her lips. She managed to sit up in bed and, as she did so, the man moved away and passed through the door at the far end of the bedroom. The lady now had the courage to get out of bed in order to follow this intruder. To her amazement, she found the door locked and bolted as she had left it earlier on. The strange man had walked straight through it! There was little doubt in her mind — she had seen a ghost.

Not wishing to alarm her servants, the lady kept quiet about the incident but, a few days later, the old man servant came to her.

'May I speak to you, my lady, about something that has been worrying me and my good wife?' he asked.

'Of course,' came the answer. 'I hope you know I will always listen to anything you come to tell me.'

'Well, it's like this, madam, these noises we have all heard from time to time. I know we have told each other it comes from rats or jackdaws but I've listened very carefully and these are not the noises of ordinary animals. We are frightened by whatever it is that makes such an eerie sound.'

The lady laughed. 'Calm yourself, William, I am sure it is nothing that cannot be explained.'

William shook his head but said no more and the lady herself, more frightened than she would admit to her servants, had another odd experience that very night. She was walking along a corridor which had a dead end when, once again, she saw the figure of the man who had disturbed her sleep previously. She advanced to meet him but he backed away and disappeared into the wall. This sort of meeting occurred so often that the lady was no longer afraid of the ghost and was interested to hear from someone in the nearby village that there was a story attached to Castell Coch. It seemed that, during the Civil War, the then master of the Castle had deposited money, silver plate and jewels in the subterranean passage leading from the Castle to that of Cardiff. This Royalist gentleman was killed in the battle against Cromwell's army and never returned to claim his treasure.

'Ah, now I know who it is I see,' said the lady to herself, 'the poor ghost comes looking for his valuable possessions.'

But although she was quite happy to live with the poor harmless ghost and the weird noises, her servants became more and more terrified. In the end, she decided to vacate the Castle, much as she loved it there. It was more important, she told herself, to keep her loyal servants who were threatening to leave her employ if she stayed.

So Castell Coch was deserted until some years later when two young men, who had also heard the story of the treasure, decided to explore the underground passage wherever it might lead and whatever it might reveal. Armed with pickaxes and torches, Glyn and Huw set out on their expedition. Down they went into the bowels of the Castle where, after a long search, they found what looked like the entrance to a passage. Inside it was dark and muddy and the water ran down the grey stone walls.

'It's creepy in here, isn't it?' said Glyn.

'We knew it would be,' replied Huw, 'but we'll be alright as long as our torches don't go out.'

On and on went the two young men. The passage seemed endless, and still there was no sign of any treasure.

'Let's go back,' suggested Huw, 'I'm very cold and there's nothing here.'

'I'm not turning back now,' replied Glyn. 'We've come too far and look, what's that ahead of us?'

As he finished speaking, there, shining through the darkness, were four bright lights. Nothing daunted, the men advanced.

'Good gracious!' exclaimed Glyn, 'they are the eyes of two eagles.'

'And they are perching on an iron chest,' added Huw. 'Glyn, we've found the treasure.'

They walked cautiously forward and, suddenly, the eagles sprang upon them, attacking them with claws and beaks.

'Turn back', cried Huw, trying to beat off the huge bird with his torch.

He and Glyn retreated hastily and the royal birds flew screaming back to the iron chest.

But the young men were not easily defeated and the next day, armed now with pistols and bullets, they sat off along the passage once again. When they came within reach of the eagles, they fired but with no effect. The eagles attacked as they had done before, this time, they beat out the torches with their powerful wings. Glyn and Huw stumbled back along the corridor; it was a long and arduous journey.

'What are we to do now?' asked Glyn. 'I don't know what else we can do.'

Huw thought for a few moments. 'How about trying silver bullets?'

'Good idea, Huw, and we'll get them blessed by a priest. In fact we'll take a priest with us.'

After some persuasion and the promise of a part of the treasure for his church, the local priest consented to go with the men and the three of them hopefully set out on the trail of the eagles and that iron chest. It was not long before the four red lights of the eagles' eyes shone out in the darkness ahead of them. The priest began to read out an exocism for surely, he thought, these birds were instruments of the devil. He was only halfway through the prayer when the eagles attacked. Glyn and Huw fired their silver bullets but these had no more effect that the ordinary bullets had had. This assault was more severe than the previous ones had been, the enraged birds attacked furiously. The men, bleeding and tired, retreated in terror, the poor priest wishing he had never consented to come with the young men. Glyn and Huw both confessed they were beaten. It was useless to try again; the eagles would never give up the treasure they so jealously guarded. And, as far as anyone knows, the eagles and the iron chest are still there beneath Castell Coch but, since Glyn and Huw, no-one has been bold enough to disturb them.

Princess Thanen and Her Son

Long, long ago in North Wales, there lived a certain king, a pagan, who had a very beautiful daughter called Thanen. She had heard many sermons from the mouths of Christian men and vowed to reject idols and become a Christian herself. She was devoted to the Blessed Virgin Mary and prayed to become as she did, pregnant by no man. At length she discovered she was about to have a child, and went to her father in order to explain to him what had happened.

'Father,' she said, 'I have news for you and I hope you will not take it amiss.'

'Speak on, child,' her father answered, 'you know you are my favourite daughter and can say nothing to me that could cause distress.'

Thanen looked him straight in the eye and boldly spoke out. 'In a few weeks' time I am to have a baby.'

The king could scarcely believe what he was hearing. He may have said that nothing his daughter could say would distress him but he had expected nothing like this. 'You are pregnant!' he roared. 'You, my own daughter dare to tell me this! Say you are lying, say it is not true.'

'Father, I am to have a baby,' repeated Thanen, her voice trembling.

'Then who is the father of the child?' asked the king, his voice cold as ice. 'He must marry you at once and, if he will not, he shall be put to the sword.'

'There is no father,' said Thanen quietly.

'What do mean *no* father? You are without chastity. Tell me the man's name.'

'There in no man,' whispered Thanen, 'only the Holy Spirit.'

'You talk like a mad woman,' thundered the king. 'If you will not confide in me, then I never wish to set eyes on you again,' and he called for some of his soldiers.

'This woman is no longer my daughter. She has sinned and she must be punished. Take her to Din-Pellder and throw her from the top of it.'

Din-Pellder was the name of a mountain in the district and is Welsh for a 'Round Mountain Far Off.'

Thanen begged for her father's understanding, holding out her arms to him, but he looked away and repeated the order to his soldiers. His lovely daughter was led away in tears.

The soldiers, although disliking the task, but not daring do disobey their king, took the princess to the summit of the mountain. They muttered among themselves, a few of them unwilling to take part in throwing the princess to her death. Thanen sighed and wept, looked up to heaven and prayed to her Christian God.

'I know what has happened to me,' she said. 'I do not want to die. I want my baby to be born and live a happy life,' and, as she spoke, her father's retainers threw her off the mountain top. But instead of falling to be dashed to pieces, she slowly slid into the valley below where she landed gently, without so much as a bruise. The soldiers watched in amazement and then scrambled down to where the princess lay, unhurt, on a grassy field. There followed some discussion as to what now they should do with her. Finally, their leader spoke.

'We cannot take the princess back to the palace. The king's wrath would be too much to bear. I suggest we take her to the sea and put her into a boat. That way we shall be rid of her, yet not directly guilty of her death.'

It was agreed that they should do this and, and after many hours' journey, they reached the ocean where they placed Thanen in a small boat, made of leather and which is called a coracle. They pushed the coracle out into the water and Thanen uttered not a word for now she felt herself safely in the hands of God; and she made no protest even though she was given no oars with which to row.

The small leather craft sailed slowly over the waves and, after many days had passed during which time Thanen became faint for lack of food and drink, it reached a creek on the Welsh side of the Bristol Channel, known in those days as the Severn Sea. There the fair princess left the boat and, on a plain between the town of Llantwit Major and the sea, in a field called Gwaun Colu, she gave birth to a son.

The next morning a certain holy man called Servanus came

across the poor, lonesome lady, cradling in her arms the newborn child.

'Oh, lady, lady,' he cried, 'blessed art though who comest in the name of the Lord.'

Thanen gave him a weak but welcoming smile. She felt safe at last.

Servanus took mother and child under his care, fed them and baptised the baby, calling him Kentigern, meaning 'First of Kings'. The boy was reared by Servanus who loved him more than any of his other companions, calling him by the poet name Muncu or 'Much Love Child', which is perhaps why the Scots later called him 'Mungo'.

For many years Thanen and her son lived peacefully with Servanus at Llantwit Major and, when the boy grew to manhood, he was a devout Christian and he travelled the land, preaching the gospel. Finally he reached Scotland and became the first Bishop of Glasgow and was afterwards known as St. Kertigern and by the Scots as St. Mungo.

The French Invasion

It was a fine day at the end of February in the year 1797 when an English gentleman who was visiting Fishguard stopped to talk to a farmer who was busy cutting the hedgerows.

'A beautiful day, sir,' commented the farmer.

'Indeed it is,' replied the gentleman. 'I am a stranger in these parts and your Welsh sunshine has been very kind to me.'

They continued to chat about the weather and were exchanging news of the day when the Englishman's attention was suddenly taken by the sight of three frigates approaching Fishguard harbour below them.

'A fine sight there,' he said, 'three of our warships sailing towards us'.

From where the men were standing there was a good view of the sea. The farmer followed the gentleman's outstretched finger. He frowned, looked away over the fields for a moment, looked back and frowned again.

'Them's no British ships,' he said.

'But they are flying our colours,' was the reply.

'Them's not British ships,' repeated the farmer.

'But how would you, a farmer, know anything about ships?' asked the Englishman.

'I haven't always been a farmer. I went to sea when I was a young man and I can tell you from the look of those frigates, they are French. I'd stake my life on it.'

'French!' exclaimed the gentleman. 'But this is terrible. You should take a horse at once and muster the soldiers. I'll go down to the harbour and see what I can find out for I speak a little French, and perhaps, after all, there is nothing to fear.'

Without more ado, the farmer ran to his stables, saddled his fastest horse and rode towards Haverfordwest where the nearest soldiers were stationed.

Meanwhile the Englishman had reached the quayside where the French troops were already beginning to land. He was not afraid, telling himself that any disagreement was between the French and the Welsh and had nothing to do with him. However, he had been enjoying his holiday and was cross that it should be spoiled in this way. He approached a French officer who was directing the troops towards the town, and spoke to him in his own tongue.

'I do not know what you are doing in this town,' he said. 'No war has been declared and I can assure you that you cannot win any battle here. Wales is a country of brave fighting men and these of Pembrokeshire are no exception.'

'We do not come as an enemy of Wales,' replied the Frenchman. 'We are here to relieve our oppressed brothers.'

'Nonsense!' snapped the Englishman. 'No one is oppressed here. The Welsh have no argument with the English in this day and age, whatever may have happened in the past.'

During this conversation, one of the French soldiers removed the silver buckles from the Englishman's shoes while two others pilfered his knee buckles. Going further into the French lines, the gentleman was approached by another French officer who accused him of being improperly dressed.

'Certainly that is so,' came the haughty reply, 'and that I am without buckles to my shoes and to my knee breeches is the fault of your rough soldiery.' He pointed to a soldier whom he recognised as being one of the thieves. 'There is one of the culprits. Do something about it.'

Somewhat taken back, the French officer sentenced the man to immediate execution but this caused such a furore among the other soldiers who declared that nothing would induce them to shoot their comrade that the officer was forced to let the thief go.

'There is not much discipline here,' said the Englishman, 'where an officer's order can so easily be disobeyed.'

The Frenchman flushed and turned away, letting the Englishman return safely to the Fishguard hotel where he was staying.

By now, the local inhabitants had become aware that the French troops had arrived in their quiet country town. At first it had been thought that the approaching vessels were merchant ships seeking safety from an approaching gale but it was not long before anxiety was changed into alarm as boats were seen of armed men putting off from the ships. By midnight the boats ceased coming; all the soldiers has disembarked. However, it was so dark that it was impossible to ascertain the number of the force. Knots of local men filled the streets to discuss the invasion and it was decided to evacuate the women and children.

Next day the men of Fishguard armed themselves with pitchforks, scythes, pistols or whatever weapons they could snatch, determined to face the foe until the militia, warned by the farmer, could arrive. The French meanwhile, hungry and tired and deserted now by the ships in which they had arrived, were busy foraging. They laid their hands upon everything eatable in the neighbourhood. A few days before, a wreck with a cargo of spirits had occurred on the coast and every cottage was supplied with a cask. Soon the French soldiers were both drunk and overfed. Such discipline as there had been was now at an end.

The local men informed the enemy that if a shot were fired, they would close in on them at once. Soon a small troop of soldiers arrived from Haverfordwest and a parley with the French took place.

'How many have you?' demanded one of the French officers.

'Two thousand cavalry and the same number of well-trained infantry,' the Welsh officer lied bravely.

The Frenchman had his doubts about the truth of this but happened to look at that moment towards the hills behind the town where the women and children had been sent. A multitude of women stood there, row upon row of them, wearing the red flannel shawls and tall beaver hats as was their custom. They had the appearance to a foreign eye of a red coated regiment of soldiers.

'By God!' exclaimed the French officer. 'Truly you do not lie. We are outnumbered. Gives us twelve hours to capitulate.'

'I'll give you as many minutes,' snapped the English officer.

At two o'clock the enemy laid down their arms. That night they were marched away as prisoners. The feeling between the French officers and their men was so bad that the officers begged to be separated from them. The officers, therefore, were sent to Carmarthen and the privates were brought to Haverfordwest. Their numbers exceeded fourteen hundred. Many of the soldiers appeared to have the marks of fetters upon their legs and it was later assumed that they were criminals of whom the French government wished to be rid. Their behaviour certainly did not bear the mark of professional soldiers.

The whole happening had been almost farcial but thus ended the last French invasion of British soil.

Vortigern and the Dragons

Long, long ago in the sixth century, there lived a great man called Vortigern, the powerful ruler of part of Britain. But he betrayed his people when he paid the false Saxons to fight for him as mercenaries. Soon these mercenaries were joined by more men like them and Vortigern's power came to an end as the whole of southern Britain was ravaged by the Saxon hordes. Vortigern fled to Wales and set about building a fortress near Dinas Emrys in Caernarfonshire. There a high rock towered from the centre of a vale, overlooking the waters of Llyn Dinas and this was the spot Vortigern chose.

He began building his stronghold, but something strange began to happen. Each day a wall was built and, by the next evening, the wall had fallen down. This happened over and over again, puzzling and plagueing Vortigern until he was finally forced to send for a local magician.

'How can it be that every stone that is laid has fallen to the ground by the following morning?' he asked.

The magician pulled at his beard, frowned and went into a reverie. He spent a long time thinking over the problem and finally he spoke.

'This is not altogether a new problem. I have known it happen in other places. There is only one way that you may construct your castle without hindrance.'

'Speak on,' urged Vortigern. 'The sooner this matter is settled, the better.'

'It is not an easy answer I can give you. It involves a certain amount of patience.'

'Go on, go on,' cried Vortigern impatiently.

'Patience, I said patience,' chided the wizard. 'You must first find a boy who was born without a father. This boy must then be sacrificed on this mountain crag and his blood sprinkled on the stones.'

'Where do I look for such a boy?' asked Vortigern.

'Look to the south,' advised the magician, and would say no more.

The boy was finally found by Vortigern's men in a small village in South Wales; his name was Emrys and he was most unwilling to travel north, suspecting what his fate would be.

'I should prefer to stay here with my mother,' said Emrys. 'She has no-one else to look after her.'

The men merely growled at him, seized him and carried him northwards. When Vortigern set eyes on the boy, who was a handsome lad and carried himself well, he was almost sorry that such a boy had to be sacrificed.

'Why am I here?' asked Emrys. 'To my knowledge I have never done you any harm.'

'I need to sprinkle your blood on the foundation stones of the castle I am building,' replied Vortigern slowly. 'There is no other way to get it built. Each day the walls are partly finished and the next day they are down. No-one can explain it and only the wizard has an answer; that is why you are here.'

'There is another answer,' said Emrys, who was not without his own brand of magic.

'How can a mere boy know such a thing?'

'There is another answer,' replied Emrys, 'Please hear me out, my lord.'

Vortigern nodded; he liked the boy and was not averse to postponing his death.

'Below the foundations of your castle there is a lake and, at the bottom of the lake, there are two dragons fighting. One dragon is white and represents the Saxons; the other is red and represents Wales. Their terrible battle has gone on for a long time and it is this that shakes down the walls of your castle every night.'

Vortigern was astounded. 'How may I believe you?' he asked.

'Did your magician give you a better explanation?' asked the boy.

'He gave me no explanation, only a cure.'

'Listen to me then; order a well to be sunk,' said Emrys, 'and find out the truth of what I say.'

Vortigern gave the order and, sure enough, the lake was found, deep below the foundation of the castle. A great roar was heard and the air became hot and steamy as the two huge

Vortigern and the Dragons

dragons rose towards the sky, their claws flailing and their teeth sunk into each other's horny flesh.

A fierce battle followed in the air, sometimes the red dragon seemed to be winning and the next moment the white one fought back and appeared to be the stronger. For hours the battle raged as Vortigern and his followers looked on in amazement. Only Emrys appeared to be unimpressed. It was, after all, only what he had expected. Finally, making an enormous effort, the red dragon overpowered the white one which fell to the ground, never to rise again. The red dragon flew off, bellowing forth flames and smoke and swishing his long tail to and fro with an air of triumph.

'Wales has won!' exclaimed Emrys, 'surely now Wales will certainly survive.'

So Vortigern built his castle without any further disasters and Emrys returned to his village in South Wales, happy that he had so narrowly escaped with his life.

The Eight Kings

It was at the end of the tenth century and Edgar was king of England while two brothers, Evan and James, jointly ruled North Wales. One day these brothers quarrelled and James had Evan thrown into prison. Howel, a son of Evan, gathered an army with the intention of setting his father free and avenging the insult his father had endured. Howel defeated his uncle James who immediately left the country and made his way to England and Edgar's court. There he addressed the king.

'I seek your help, my lord. I have been driven out of my own country by a treacherous nephew.'

King Edgar interrupted him. 'I understand that you are not wholly without blame.'

'I sire?' Not I, sire,' denied James.

'Did you not put your brother Evan in prison? Is that not the truth?'

James cast down his eyes and, realising there was no point in denying the fact, he said nothing but merely nodded his head.

'Why have you come to me?' asked Edgar, 'knowing that your country and mine are so often at war?'

'I want nothing but peace,' said James, 'I need your help to invade my country and thus regain my rightful position.'

After some apparent deliberation, King Edgar agreed to James's request. Indeed, he was glad to have the opportunity of having a voice in Welsh affairs. He marched with his army with James at his side.

Under safe conduct, the rebel Howel proceeded to the camp of Edgar where he faced his uncle James. At first they refused to speak, glowering at each other, while James muttered under his breath.

'Come now,' said Edgar, 'let us have no more of this bad feeling. You are blood relations and some agreement should be reached between you.'

'What is expected of me?' asked Howel.

'That you should let your uncle James return here to rule his people.'

'I'll agree on one condition only,' said Howel.

'No conditions,' cried James. 'I return as the king of my country.'

'You were only ever *joint* king with your brother,' Edgar reminded him and then he turned to Howel, 'What is your condition?'

'That I rule with my uncle in place of my father Evan.'

'Why should I agree to that,' said James angrily. He addressed Edgar. 'My nephew chased me out of Wales: we are enemies.'

'You *were* enemies,' said Edgar wearily. These Welsh, he told himself, are a quarrelsome lot. 'If you cannot agree with each other, then I shall take over your kingdom and rule it myself.'

James and Howel looked at each other. Howel forced a smile and, grudgingly James smiled back.

'I agree,' said James. Howel held out the hand of friendship and, somewhat unwillingly, James grasped it.

Edgar then invited them to join him at his court in Chester, to which they agreed. The King of England had also invited six other so-called kings from various parts of Wales. Perhaps it was his intention to show them the meaning of unity; these pretensions of petty chiefs seem to have amused Edgar; at any rate he had an unusual request to make of them.

'I have a royal barge here,' he said 'and I propose that you eight kings shall row me on the river Dee from Chester to the monastery of St. John the Baptist and row back again after divine service in the chapel of this monastery. What say you to this plan?'

Although he asked the question, Edgar was really issuing an order. Seven of the kings agreed to obey his request but the eighth, a man called Gwaithvoed, a name meaning 'May be by a Warrior', spoke out.

'I refuse to act as a servant to any king, and certainly I will not obey a king of England.'

'Those are harsh words,' smiled Edgar who secretly admired this king for his proud spirit.

'Maybe that is so but I would say to you, fear him who fears not death,' came the reply.

114

'There is no question of my issuing you an order to die,' Edgar assured him. 'You are free to go your way.'

The royal barge needed eight men to row it, four rowers on each side of Edgar but, as there were now only seven men, King Edgar himself became the eighth man. The seven kings were all laughing and apparently enjoyed the joke Edgar had played on them.

The proud king Gwaithvoed was from near Cardiff and all his descendents ever since the episode at Chester, retained the words 'Fear him who fears not death' as their family motto. Before he departed for South Wales, Edgar went to see him, greeted him with great cordiality, gave him his hand and courteously said, 'I desire only to be your friend and friend to all of your kindred and of your subjects.'

Princess Gwenllian

Gruffyth, son of King Rhys ap Tudor, was brought up at the court of Ireland but, when he reached the age of twenty-one, he had an urge to return to the land of his birth. He went to live with his half sister, Princess Nesta de Windsor at Pembroke Castle, and there he stayed for a couple of years. Henry I was King of England at the time and was suspicious that Gruffyth had intentions of seizing the throne of North Wales. To escape Henry's clutches, Gruffyth left Pembroke hastily and made his way to Anglesey and the court there of Gruffyth ap Cynan, who we will call ap Cynan to avoid confusion.

Gruffyth had just arrived after a long journey and was seated at table, being refreshed with food and drink when King ap Cynan entered the hall. At his side Gruffyth saw a most beautiful young woman, slender as a willow sapling, her red-gold hair showering to her shoulders and her skin flushed like a ripe peach.

'Allow me, cousin, to present to you my daughter Gwenllian,' said ap Cynan.

For a few moments Gruffyth could scarcely speak, so overcome was he by the lady's beauty.

He rose from the table and Gwenllian held out her slim hand which he took and gently kissed.

'Madam,' he said, 'I am, and always will be, your faithful servant.'

Gwenllian smiled and her bright blue eyes met the dark brown ones of Gruffyth. It was love at first sight.

Meanwhile Henry had learned where Gruffyth was now residing and, to the surprise of ap Cynan, he invited this king of a small part of Wales to stay with him at Windsor Castle. Never before had ap Cynan received such a gesture from so great a king.

'My daughter, this is a wonderful chance to see the splendour of an English court, and I would have you accompany me,' said ap Cynan.

Gwenllian did not want to leave Gruffyth but, in spite of her tears, her father insisted that he must have her company.

'Gwenllian, do not weep,' said Gruffyth. 'You will not be long away and, when you return, we will speak of our marriage and hope that your father will approve of it.'

Gwenllian dried her eyes and managed a weak smile when Gruffyth took her in his arms and kissed away the tears.

At Henry's court, ap Cynan and his daughter were given a warm welcome and, at first, both were unaware that Henry wanted Gruffyth as his prisoner and hoped to achieve this by flattering ap Cynan in the fashion of a tiger licking an antelope before making a meal of it.

'I should be greatly pleased with you, Cynan, if you would deliver into my hands this said Gruffyth, son of King Rhys,' said Henry.

'Lord, I will do anything that you command,' replied the treacherous ap Cynan.

But both kings were unaware that the quiet Princess Gwenllian heard much of what was said between Henry and her father. She kept a careful watch over them both and, one night, when she was alone with her father, she tried to learn from him exactly what Henry and he had planned. Ap Cynan drank more wine than was good for him. It was a good moment for Gwenllian to discover the truth of what she already suspected.

'What does king Henry want of you?' she asked. 'Surely he did not bring you here so that you might enjoy the hospitality of his magnificent court.'

Cynan mumbled that indeed that was the only reason why he had been invited.

'That is nonsense,' exclaimed Gwenllian, pouring more wine into his goblet. The more drunk he was, she guessed, the more likely was she to learn the truth.

'Come now, father,' she coaxed. 'We both know Henry has an ulterior motive.' She put her arms around her father's neck. 'You can tell me. I am well able to keep a secret.'

'Well I'm not sure I should confide in you,' muttered Cynan. 'But I suppose I can trust you.'

'Yes, yes, father,' urged Gwenllian. 'Tell me has it anything to do with my beloved Gruffyth.'

'Yes, that is so; you must be brave, my daughter, and forget your love for this Gruffyth. King Henry intends . . .' Here Cynan stopped to drink another goblet of wine.

'Go on, go on, go on,' urged Gwenllian, who was now thoroughly alarmed.

'King Henry,' went on ap Cynan, 'wants me to deliver into his hands, Gruffyth, son of Rhys ap Tudor. He fears this young man is getting too much power in North Wales and may not be too friendly towards an English king. He, he . . .'

Here ap Cynan stopped, his head fell on the table top and, bemused by the wine, he went to sleep.

Gwenllian had to think quickly. Among her servants was one who could be trusted and who was as at home on his horse as he was on his feet. She sent for him and told him to make haste from Windsor to North Wales where he was to inform Gruffyth of the danger in which he was. On hearing this news from the faithful messenger, Gruffyth made his way speedily to a monastery at Aberdaron at the extreme north of Wales. He was received into sanctuary at a monastery where the good monks welcomed him and promised to give him any help he might need.

It was not long before Gwenllian and her father returned to their home in Aberfraw. Ap Cynan was surprised and upset to find that Gruffyth had left. Gwenllian pretended she, too, was surprised but she was inwardly delighted to know her sweetheart had received her message.

When ap Cynan had recovered from the shock, and since he was eager to be a friend of King Henry, he gathered together a troop of cavalry and, staying at home himself, sent them to the Aberdaron sanctuary. One of his servants, overhearing some conversation between Gwenllian and her loyal messenger, had learnt that Aberdaron was protecting Gruffyth and had told this news to his master ap Cynan.

The monks of Aberdaron, seeing the army of cavalry approaching, went out to meet them, singing a Georgian chant, with the Prior carrying aloft the cross. Overawed by this peaceful and religious welcome, the soldiers were ashamed, got down from their horses, put down their weapons and bowed reverently to the cross. They then turned round and went back to ap Cynan's palace at Aberfraw.

When ap Cynan was told that Gruffyth was under the protection of the cross in the sanctuary of Aberdaron, he knew he could do no more. Gwenllian, of course, could hardly conceal her joy.

Gruffyth now realised that it was not safe for him to remain in North Wales. Henry would not rest until he was captured. So, one night, in total darkness, he and a few monks left Aberdaron and made their way by sea, crossing Cardigan bay and finally reaching Swansea bay. Gruffyth settled nearby in the green wood of Penll'r Gaer, together with a few of the faithful monks, without whose help he could never have managed that long trip by sea. One or two of these monks made their way back to Aberfraw to tell the good news to Gwenllian.

She was a lady of spirit and intelligence and, since she was in no danger, she was able to make her way to the south and into the arms of her lover.

The wedding of this princely pair did not take place in a fine cathedral and there was little pomp and ceremony, nor a wedding feast with singing and dancing.

'I wish Gwenllian, my love,' said Gruffyth, 'that we could have had a wedding more fitting for a princess.'

'The leafy sacred oaks overhead are as fine a ceiling as that of any cathedral' replied Gwenllian, 'and this faithful monk who is to conduct our wedding is as noble as any bishop. We are man and wife and my simple ring of entwined grass is all I shall ever need.'

The Death of Princess Gwenllian

The happy days Gwenllian and Gruffyth spent in the green wood of Penll'r Gaer, where Gruffyth had by now built a splendid palace, were to last only a few years. It was not long before Gruffyth had surrounded himself with an army of men loyal to him and began to attack the English forces wherever they happened to be in Wales.

Gwenllian had borne twin sons, Maelgwn and Morgan and, when they were nine years old, their father called his wife and children to the great hall of his fortress where he had recently been discussing plans with his senior officers. Now he was alone and looked sad when he gave them the news of what was happening in Wales.

'I want to explain to you why I must leave you, even if for only a short time.'

'Cannot we come with you wherever you go?' asked Gwenllian who had never been separated before from her husband.

'Battle fields are no places for women and children,' replied Gruffyth. 'I am going to see your father, Gwenllian,' he continued. 'I know ap Cynan and we have not always been friends. He resented my marriage to you but all is forgiven and forgotten and I must seek his help to fight the English Normans who have seized so much of our land.'

'We are not children, father,' said Morgan. 'We could fight by your side.'

'Not children!' said Gruffyth, smiling. 'Not children at nine years old. No, my lad, you and Maelgwn must wait a few more years before fighting at my side.'

'But, my lord,' interrupted Gwenllian, 'I should dearly love to see my father again. Could I not come with you?'

'Too dangerous,' replied Gruffyth, 'and, anyway, you are needed here to look after the children and to take my place as general in command. I shall leave some men here to guard you. The rest must come with me. The Englishman Lord Maurice de Londres has a garrison at Kidwelly Castle nearby. He will attack us as soon as he has reinforcements but not before I have returned with extra men provided by your father to protect us.'

'What if Lord Maurice should attack before you return?' asked a worried Gwenllian.

'He'll not do that,' reassured Gruffyth, 'he hasn't enough men.' Little did he know how wrong he was proved to be.

He bade Gwenllian and his twin sons, embracing them and assuring them that he would not be long away. So his wife and children were left at home to cope with the trouble that lay ahead.

One unhappy day, one of Gwenllian's messengers came to her with alarming news.

'My lady,' he said, his voice and body tired from running a great distance. 'It seems that Lord Maurice's hoped for reinforcements have arrived from England, crossing the Bristol Channel, landing here in Glamorgan and already on their way to Kidwelly Castle. With my lord Gruffyth absent with most of his men, we can hardly withstand any invasion from Lord Maurice and the increased number of men he is expecting at any moment.'

Gwenllian was greatly upset to hear this terrible news but, with Gruffyth away in the north, she knew she must now take charge of the situation. She summoned to her the few officers her husband had left behind.

'It seems Lord Maurice's reinforcements have not yet reached Kidwelly Castle so our first duty is to go there before his extra men arrive and attack him before he attacks us.'

Her officers were not sure this was good strategy but they obeyed immediately and mustered their soldiers, recognising their lady's bravery and authority.

Gwenllian, ordering her troops to advance, rode at their head, having her twin sons on ponies either side of her. Unfortunately, she soon found herself and her army in between the forces of Kidwelly Castle and those who had come across the Channel to join Lord Maurice. At night, the Princess struck camp but at dawn she realised the peril in which she found herself with Lord Maurice ahead of her and his English supporters behind her.

It was not long before Maurice's troops attacked and

Gwenllian found herself in the midst of fighting warriors, those of hers and those of Lord Maurice and his reinforcements. Like Boadicea long before her, like a tigress at bay, Gwenllian urged on her men with loud cries and expensive gestures. Suddenly she felt an extreme stab of pain in her shoulder and she fell, wounded, from her horse. Little Maelgwn, one of the twins, thew himself down at his mother's side and tried to protect her from further blows.

'Mother,' he wailed, 'Mother please do not die.' But his words faded away as an arrow hit him in the chest and he lay dead, sprawled across his mother's body. Gwenllian, severely wounded was, nonetheless, still alive but was unable to get to her feet. Her whole army was soon defeated, the odds against them too great. Gwenllian and Morgan, the other twin, were soon captured. Gwenllian lying on a rough litter and Morgan stumbling at her side, they were taken to Kidwelly Castle.

Lord Maurice de Londres now eternally disgraced his name by ordering that the heroic Gwenllian and her brave little son Morgan be instantly beheaded in his presence. Thus, a princess, who was descended from a long line of ancient kings, and her remaining son were killed. Gwenllian made no plea for mercy and Morgan had cried his only tears at the death of his twin and went to his death with an air of pride and dignity. The scene of this barbarous event is still known by the name of 'Maes Gwenllian' or 'Gwenllian's Fenceless Field.'

When the terrible news of these events reached the ears of Gruffyth, he instantly returned to South Wales at the head of 2,000 horsemen and 6,000 foot soldiers. The entire country was aghast at the fate of so sweet a princess and so small a boy. With Gruffyth commanding them, the soldiers sacked and destroyed the castles of Aberystwyth, Dinerth, Caerwerdros and Cardigan. Popular resentment was so intense that the Welshmen drove nearly all of the Normans out of South Wales. Thus were the sad deaths of the princess and her twin sons revenged.

Sadly, only a few months later, Gruffyth, his heart broken and overcome by grief, himself died, not in his great palace but in the willow cabin at Penll'r Gaer where he and Gwenllian had been married and where they had been so happy together.

Alice

It was towards the end of the 19th century when Alice and her sisters Lorina and Edith Liddell sat in the sitting room of a house called Pen Morfa in Llandudno where they and their parents stayed each summer. On this particular day it was raining hard and the three little girls were chatting away to each other in order to pass the time. Edith and Lorina were lively little girls and were playing happily with their dolls whilst Alice with her long straight hair was talking to them now and then but mainly gazed out of the window, dreaming dreams, and longing for the rain to stop so that she might wander over the sand dunes on the West shore where she could hitch up her cumbersome clothes and paddle in the warm clear sea.

'We are having a visitor tonight,' announced Edith suddenly.

'Who's coming?' asked Lorina. 'One of Papa's boring friends?'

Mr. Liddell was Dean of Christchurch, Oxford, a serious man who had once written a history of Ancient Rome which none of his three daughters found at all interesting.

'It's that quiet man who blushes and stammers,' Edith replied. 'You know who I mean, that mathematics man. I heard Mama mention it this morning.'

'Not Mr. Dodgson!' exlaimed Alice. 'Why he's quite my favourite of Papa's friends. How long is he staying?'

'About a week, I think,' said Edith. 'But I don't know what you see in him, he's so shy.'

'He tells the most wonderful stories,' said Alice. 'I could listen to him all day long.'

'Men who know only about arithmetic and Algebra and all that cannot possibly tell stories that would appeal to us.'

'You're wrong,' replied Alice quietly, 'quite, quite wrong.'

Mr. Dodgson arrived that evening just in time to see the three girls before they went to bed. His conversation with Dean Liddell and his wife had been very one-sided as the visitor seemed unable to say much to them. They were a very kind couple and tried hard to make him feel at home, but he had scarcely uttered one word and sat now quietly smoking his pipe in a corner of the room where he could not easily be seen but, when the children appeared in their pretty lace trimmed nightgowns, he moved forward to see them better and his eyes lit up when he saw what appeared to be three little angels, although their father disillusioned Mr. Dodgson, saying they were more like little devils most of the time. But he smiled as he said it and no-one took offence. The children lined up to kiss their parents goodnight and almost immediately Mr. Dodgson began to talk to them and stammered but a little as he spoke. It was Alice who talked back. Lorina and Edith were not so impressed with this stange young man even though he did produce some delicious chocolates from inside the pocket where he normally kept his pipe.

'Do you remember, Alice, that lovely day when we were together on the river at Oxford?' asked Mr. Dodgson.

Alice remembered it well for it had been a most marvellous day when he had told her some marvellous stories.

As Mr. Dodgson went on chatting easily with the children, he now produced from the same large pocket some puzzles and a few small toys. He knew exactly the games and toys the children most enjoyed and they went to bed, happy with their new gifts.

'There you see,' said Alice once she was in bed, 'I told you Mr. Dodgson is a very nice, kind man.'

Her two sisters nodded their small, sleepy heads and admitted that Alice was right. Even so, the next day Edith and Lorina preferred to go for a drive in the pony and trap with their mother and father while Alice said she would prefer to go for a walk with Mr. Dodgson. They made their way towards the sand hills and rabbit warrens where they sat down and munched some sweets which the young man produced from the same pocket which had revealed such a wonderful supply of interesting things the night before.

'Mr. Dodgson,' said Alice as soon as they had settled down, 'will you please tell me a story with plenty of nonsense in it?'

Mr. Dodgson smiled his shy smile. 'All my stories have plenty of nonsense in them. Look over there, Alice, can you see that little rabbit scuttling away over the sand dunes?'

Alice followed his pointing finger and nodded her head.

'Then let's have a story about a rabbit. How about that?'

'Oh yes, please please and could I be in the story with the rabbit?'

'That is possible,' said Mr. Dodgson, trying to look very serious. 'Here begins the story of Alice and the white rabbit. "Alice was beginning to get very tired . . ." '

'But I'm not at all tired,' protested Alice.

'For the purpose of this story,' said her friend, 'you are very tired so please do not interrupt me again.' He sounded cross but, at the same time, he winked at Alice and pulled a funny face which made her laugh.

'But that wasn't a white rabbit we saw,' interupted Alice again. 'It was an ordinary brown rabbit.'

'There will be nothing ordinary about my rabbit,' Mr. Dodgson assured her. And he began to tell the little girl a most extraordinary story. He was nowhere near the end of it when he looked at his watch and said it was high time they went home for luncheon.

Edith and Lorina were so busy telling Alice what they had seen on their ride that they were not as interested as Alice would like them to have been when she told them about Mr. Dodgson's story.

'It is the most wonderful story and he is going to continue it tomorrow,' said Alice, 'and then you can hear it, too.'

But when the next morning came, although all three little girls went for a walk with their visitor, Lorina and Edith went to look for shells on the beach while Alice settled down to listen to more of Mr. Dodgson's remarkable story, a bubbling delight of strange characters who did very strange things. Each day Alice listened, entranced, as the tale continued until finally, and before it was finished, the Liddell's guest departed and returned to Oxford where he lived.

Now there was something special about those walks with Mr. Dodgson, something special about Alice Liddell and something very special about the story. Alice was made the heroine of the fictional 'Alice in Wonderland', a book that is perhaps the most famous of all children's books and it was written by a man called Lewis Carroll, whose real name was Dodgson, and the inspiration had come to him during his stay in Llandudno.

Many, years later, in 1933, a famous Welsh politician unveiled a memorial to Lewis Carroll, a statue of the White Rabbit and some of the immortal characters who lived in this magical of books. So many children have paid a visit to this statue to shake the paw of the White Rabbit that it actually fell off a few years later.

Let us leave the last word to Mr. Lloyd George who said, 'Lewis Carroll radiates happiness and the world today is a happier place because he passed through it. It is great thing for you in Llandudno to know that he drew inspiration from your sea and your mountains and that it was the hand of a little child who led him.'

Prince Madoc

Most people if asked who discovered America would reply 'Christopher Columbus, of course' but there are some Welshmen who would not agree with this, saying that Prince Madoc, son of Owain Gwyneth who owned land in North Wales, discovered America at least two centuries before Columbus. Now follows the kind of story that might have happened.

Thomas, son of a lord who served Madoc, was nearly fourteen when his father sent for him to discuss his future.

'You know that Madoc takes a great interest in you, my boy,' said Thomas's father, 'and I have a suggestion to make with which you may agree or disagree, as you please. You know I have never forced you to anything you did not want to do.'

Thomas was puzzled; his father appeared both serious and a little troubled.

'I'll do anything you ask of me, father,' he said.

'Perhaps, son, it would be better if you talked to Prince Madoc himself and not to me,' suggested his father.

So Thomas went to see the prince who had a high regard for Thomas's father.

'Father said I should talk to you about something, sire, which apparently he does not wish to discuss with me.'

Madoc smiled. 'Well, boy, you are nearly a man now and, as you know, I am as happy at sea as on land, unlike most Welshmen who have no reputation for being good sailors. I am taking two ships to explore a far land across the Atlantic Ocean.'

'Across the Ocean!' exclaimed Thomas, 'but surely, if you sail to the west, our ships will go over the edge of the world and that would be the end of them.'

Madoc laughed. 'That is a foolish attitude to take. The world I believe to be round. It is only landlubbers who think otherwise.'

'But what is all this to do with me anyway?' asked Thomas.

'I'll come straight to the point, I should like you to be part of my crew. I have spoken to your father about this and he has reluctantly agreed that you should come with me, but only if you wish to do so.'

Thomas was so astounded by these words that for a moment he could think of nothing to say.

'Come, come, boy, make up your mind quickly. I have little time for trivial conversation nor for your silence. Just let me say I should like your answer.'

'But why me?' asked Thomas.

'Because of the regard I have for your father who has always been a man of courage and intelligence and I hope some of this will have rubbed off on you.'

'But why not ask my father to go with you then, instead of me?'

'He is too old, and anyway I do not necessarily need an experienced sailor. I want a boy like you to help the cook, to scrub the decks and to wait on me. I'll have you on my ship, not on the other ship accompanying me, but where I can keep a friendly eye on you. Now what do you think?'

'I should love it,' said Thomas instantly. 'It will be the most exciting thing I have ever done and I am truly grateful that you ask me to go with you. I go with you wherever you may sail, and if there is land beyond the Atlantic Ocean, who knows what treasure we may find.'

'It is land, not treasure I am looking for, my lad. There is so much to be learned about the new world and to be the first westerner to find such a place would mean as much to me as a thousand pieces of gold.'

A few weeks went by until the ships of Madoc were ready to sail, weeks during which Thomas became more and more excited at the thought of the adventure which lay ahead of him. However, when the day arrived to set sail from Aber-Cerrig-Gwynion near Rhos-on-Sea, Thomas began to have butterflies in his stomach. The ships were primitive compared to our modern standards, being made of wood with sails of canvas and some with oars to help them on their way. The ship Prince Madoc commanded and on which Thomas worked was called Gwenna Garn or, in English Horn Gwenna.

In 1170, the day on which they sailed was balmy and the sea calm and blue. Thomas was sure he was going to enjoy the long journey ahead but, alas, when they had been out at sea for only a couple of days, the weather changed. The wind arose and the sea became turbulent with great waves sweeping over the deck of the ship. Thomas began to feel very ill but still tried to carry out his duties. He was sickened by the sight of the food he had to prepare for Madoc and his officers. He could scarcely stand on his feet to sweep the deck and, at night, the swinging of the hammock in which he slept was such that he was often unable to get any sleep at all.

Many months went by and poor Thomas felt no better. At last Madoc cried out in triumph.

'Look, look, there is land just ahead; look, you must look!'

Captain and crew were elated but Thomas was beyond caring except that the thought of his feet on dry land instead of the nightmare he had been enduring was something to be welcomed. The two ships docked in a place that was later to be named Mobile Bay, in Alabama. As soon as Thomas was able to leave the ship, he shouted with joy when he left the vessel which had hardly been very kind to him, or so he thought.

Many more months went by as Madoc and his crew settled in the lush countryside where fish were easily caught and birds and deer killed by the archer's bow. One day, a few strange people arrived silently in what was now Madoc's settlement. They looked savage, with their faces painted bright colours, but their approach was gentle. They were members of a race which was later mistakenly called Red Indian and this particular tribe was known as the Mandans. Thomas was astonished to learn that such a primitive people should know as much as these Mandans knew. They could follow trails, were efficient with the bow and arrow, treated their wives well and lived in tents that were better than many of the hovels Thomas had seen at home in Wales.

Thomas had just begun to enjoy himself, learning some words of the Mandan language and, in return teaching them some words of Welsh, when Madoc announced that it was time to leave and make for home, to tell his wonderful story of the new country he had found to his fellow Welshmen. There were calm days and stormy days when it seemed the ship might sink and the story never told. Thomas felt better on the return journey than he had felt when they had first set out on the adventure. The journey that today would take only a matter of hours took, in the year 1170, over a year, and when the ships arrived back

129

at what is now call Port Madoc, there was great excitement among local lords and the ordinary country folk, all of whom had been convinced they would never again see Madoc and his sailors. All Thomas was able to say to his father was, 'I had never known such a wonderful place as America could ever have existed. We saw only a tiny bit of it but there must be miles and miles of it still undiscovered. I would not have missed such an experience and shall remember it to my dying day.'

But his attitude changed when, some time later, Madoc sent for him again.

'Now young Thomas, you are more of a man than the boy I first took on our voyage of discovery, are you not? Well, I am sailing again. Are you coming with me?'

Thomas was silent and Madoc repeated his question. This time Thomas blushed and Madoc let out a cry of surprise.

'Do you not wish to see again what we witnessed last time?'

'It's not that, sire, not that,' mumbled Thomas.

Madoc grinned. 'You need go no further; I know what troubles you. You liked the destination but hated the journey. Am I right?'

Thomas hung his head and agreed that this was so. He could never forget those months of hardship. It was with some regret, however, that he saw Madoc set sail without him.

Madoc was never seen again in Wales but it is possible that he safely reached the shores of Alabama once more, and that he and his men mixed with the Indian Mandan tribe. For example, it is certain that the Mandan tribe, which died out in the last century, possessed words in the language which appeared to be Welsh and, unlike other Red Indians, there were some of them bearded and blue-eyed. Whether we believe the story of Madoc and his ships or are sceptical of the whole story, it is interesting to note that, as recently as 1953, a Ladies' Society called 'Daughters of Revolution' actually erected a memorial tablet at Fort Morgan, Mobile Bay, Alabama, bearing these words:

'In memory of Prince Madoc, a Welsh explorer, who landed on the shores of Mobile Bay, Alabama, in 1170 and left behind, with the Indians, the Welsh language.'

130

The Buccaneer

Unlike Madoc, Henry Morgan was a landsman rather than a seaman, even though he is thought of as one of the great pirates of his age. He was born at Tredegar in South Wales, the son of a landowner, in the year 1655. He was of average height but burly and pictures of him show him to have had a typical Welsh bullet head. He was handsome in a bold way, good eyes, straight nose and full-lipped mouth. As was the fashion, he wore a flowing wig and had a moustache and small beard.

As a young man, he had a sense of adventure which took him from a luxurious home to Cardiff and from there to Bristol where he heard lurid tales of some of the men of the Caribbean and the gold and jewels which they plundered. He joined a ship, brimming with a sense of spirit and ambition. He had a hard time on board but worse was to come. The ship foundered and Henry was captured, taken to Barbados and sold as a bondsman.

Morgan was a born leader and escaped from bondage with a band of other slaves as ruthless as he was himself. The image of a pirate is often of someone romantic and brave. Morgan certainly had enormous courage but gathered around him an army of ruffians who, like him, would stop at nothing. They fought; they plundered; they looted. French and Spanish ships alike were good targets for rich picking. The profits were huge and, at the height of his success, Morgan was ordered to return to England to face charges of bad behaviour. There he met and so charmed King Charles that he was made governor of Jamaica and was knighted into the bargain. No doubt some of his profits went into the royal coffers in return for these favours. Henry had risen to great heights.

He was too restless a spirit to stay quietly in Jamaica. His sights were now set on the wealth that could be found in Panama where he had his eyes on the capture of a Spanish galleon sailing with a cargo of treasure and a few passengers. The figure of the treasure was said to amount to millions of pieces of eight. This particular galleon was never, in fact, conquered although

Morgan had commissioned four of the best ships for the expedition. Henry blamed the men in charge for their failure owing to their gluttony and drunkenness, several rich wines having been found on the ship. In desperation, the band of rogues found a smaller merchant vessel just arrived in Tobago whose cargo was fairly valuable. The buccaneers also raided Tobaga Island, taking prisoners a number of refugees and many slaves.

Sir Henry Morgan was a cruel man who behaved appallingly to his military enemies and the civilians whom he captured. However, there is one tale about him which shows he had a modicum of gallant chivalry, and this occurred soon after the capture of that particular Spanish galleon. Most women prisoners usually had a very hard time from Morgan and his army. But more noble women were given better treatment in the hope that a ransom might be raised for their release.

Among the women captured at Tobago was the wife of a merchant, going to join her husband in Peru. She is not named in history but we shall call her Maria. Maria was a lady of quality, virtuous, young and extremely beautiful. When Morgan first saw her, his usual hard character warmed and softened. He had her brought to the patio of his residence, a place of tiled walks, flowering shrubs and plants about a fountain with parrots swinging on hoops and tortoises near a pool. Sunlight streamed between the leaves and Sir Henry Morgan hoped that these lovely surroundings would have a good effect on Maria. He said little to her but gazed at her amorously and hoped the garden would impress her. She said even less and appeared to take no notice of her surroundings. She held herself erectly and faced her captor with fearless eyes.

'I will give you anything you desire,' said Henry at last.

'My freedom,' replied Maria coldly.

'That, madam, alas is the one thing I cannot grant.'

'Then there is no more to be said between us,' came the disdainful reply.

'Oh yes, there is indeed, I wish you to have a room in my palace and a negro woman to look after your every need.'

'It would suit me better to be left with the other prisoners,' retorted Maria.

Morgan smiled at her. She was a real beauty, this one, and with spirit, too. Maria did not smile back.

Morgan ignored her request and, true to his word, placed Maria in one of the best rooms in his palatial house with not only a negro woman to look after her but many other servants, too. She had every comfort and the best food and wines the house could supply. Every day Morgan visited her, paying her lavish compliments and anxious to please her in every way. She never replied to anything he said except when, on one occasion, she asked him to leave her alone as she was at her prayers. Morgan left without a murmur.

One day, he came back to her with a very special question.

'Madam', he said, 'I have gazed upon your beauty and admired your virtue. To be honest, I wish to marry you.'

Maria was aghast. 'Sir Henry Morgan', she replied coldly and with dignity, 'may I remind you I am already married.'

'Oh we can forget about that merchant in Peru; he is of no importance. We can be happy together without thinking of him.'

'And do we also forget a certain Mary Elizabeth in Jamaica to whom, I understand, you are already married?'

Morgan flushed for it was true what she had said. 'Yes', he replied boldly, 'we may forget about her, too.'

After a few days had elapsed and still Maria would scarcely speak to him, Morgan lost patience. Indeed Maria had said she would rather kill herself than marry him. So the Governor of Jamaica cast the poor lady into a dark and stinking prison with only rats for company and allowed her the minimum of food and water. Maybe he hoped she would now give in to his proposal but her gaolers reported that the lady spent her days in prayer and never asked to see Sir Henry. Then, having failed to make Maria change her mind, he dispatched her to join her sisters in some more comfortable accommodation and named the price of her ransom to a higher figure.

Maria assured her friends that she thought no harm would come to them as long as the ransoms asked were paid. Maria had been brought up to believe like every other Spanish lady that buccaneers were heretical and scarcely human.

'But', she said, 'I have heard this Sir Henry Morgan curse in the name of God so I believe he must be a Christian.'

Finally, she was allowed, like the other high-born women, to send messengers into the interior to find her husband.

'I am sending two of my men to collect ransom for your freedom,' said Sir Henry when next he demanded to see her.

Alas for Maria, the next time she saw him, Morgan had to say, 'I regret, madam, that my men have stolen the money your husband sent for you. They will, of course, be severely punished for this.'

For the first time Maria broke down and wept. Morgan's heart was softened at the sight of her tears.

'Why do you weep? I have already offered you my protection,' he said.

'I cannot hope to raise another ransom,' she replied. 'My husband had sent as much as he could afford. There can be no more money forthcoming.'

'Do you suppose I will make you suffer for the rascality of two thieves,' said Morgan softly, realising at last that Maria had no intention of marrying him.

He had a horse brought to her and wished her well for the journey.

'You are free as you have always wished to be,' he said.

She smiled at him for the first and last time. She was small and slim, an olive skinned beauty with glossy black hair. She rode the horse with the grace of a Spanish woman in the saddle. The hoofs of her horse clattered on the pebbles, the silver bells on its trappings jingled as she went. Morgan watched her go; he actually wiped tears from his eyes. He lifted his hand in farewell to the woman he loved. Maria did not even turn her head to acknowledge what was probably the most generous act in his life of this famous Welshman, cruel but brave Sir Henry Morgan.